T0323738

Trade Policy Disaster

The Ohlin Lectures

See http://mitpress.mit.edu for a complete list of titles in this series.

Trade Policy Disaster

Lessons from the 1930s

Douglas A. Irwin

The MIT Press
Cambridge, Massachusetts
London, England

This book was set in Palatino by Graphic Composition, Inc., Bogart, Georgia.

Library of Congress Cataloging-in-Publication Data

Irwin, Douglas A., 1962–
Trade policy disaster : lessons from the 1930s / Douglas A. Irwin.
    p.   cm. — (The Ohlin lectures)
Includes bibliographical references and index.
ISBN 978-0-262-01671-1 (hardcover : alk. paper)
ISBN 978-0-262-55383-4 (paperback)
1. Commercial policy—History. 2. Protectionism—History. 3. Free trade—History. 4. Foreign exchange rates—History. I. Title.
HF1411.I753   2012
382'.309043—dc23

                                                        2011016638

148779642

Contents

Preface

More than eighty years ago, the world experienced a deep and prolonged economic contraction that left disastrous political and social consequences in its wake. Today, the Great Depression of the 1930s remains a fascinating subject of general and scholarly interest, one that has left a permanent imprint on modern economics. As Ben Bernanke (1995, 1) once remarked,

To understand the Great Depression is the Holy Grail of macroeconomics. Not only did the Depression give birth to macroeconomics as a distinct field of study, but also—to an extent that is not always fully appreciated—the experience of the 1930s continues to influence macroeconomists' beliefs, policy recommendations, and research agendas.

The same is true for trade policy. This period of extreme duress saw an unprecedented outbreak of protectionism. The proliferation of higher tariffs, import quotas, and foreign exchange controls all contributed to the collapse of international trade. These import restrictions, combined with preferential trade blocs, destroyed the open, nondiscriminatory world trading system. Once imposed, the trade barriers took root and proved difficult to remove, stifling world trade and hindering economic recovery for years to come. In fact, it took decades of negotiations after World War II, through the General Agreement on Tariffs and Trade (GATT), before these barriers were fully unraveled.

The trade policy experience of the 1930s continues to influence the beliefs and policy recommendations of international trade economists. The worst nightmare of every trade economist is that, in the midst of an economic crisis, policymakers might be tempted to return to the autarkic, beggar-my-neighbor protectionism of the Great Depression. Such a move, it is feared, could easily spin out of control, with countries retaliating against one another in a race to close their markets to foreign goods. Not only would this destroy trade and make the crisis even worse but, if history is any guide, it would be very difficult to reverse the policies and undo the damage.

Consequently, economists frequently warn of the dangers of protectionism and criticize the use of trade policy interventions as costly and counterproductive, often by invoking the 1930s experience as an example. But they have done so without fully understanding why policymakers felt it necessary to adopt such policies at the time. For example, economists usually attribute protectionist measures to domestic producers pressuring the government for relief from foreign competition, but this was not the main story in the 1930s. Import penetration began declining for most countries when the Great Depression hit because trade fell much faster than production. Pressures from foreign competition were easing, not intensifying, for most domestic producers, although producers were still struggling to cope with falling prices and contracting demand.

Hence, the standard explanation for the existence of trade restrictions—special interest politics—does not help us understand the trade policy developments of the 1930s very well. This is problematic. If economists lack a clear understanding of why countries so easily slid into protectionism in the past, it will be difficult to recognize situations in which protectionist policies might be enacted in the future.

This book examines the trade policy disaster of the 1930s in the hope of understanding the logic behind the policy response. Once we uncover the reasons why countries resorted to protectionism, once we recover the historical context in which policymakers were willing to sacrifice open trade for other policy objectives, we will be in a better position to draw lessons that can help us avoid making similar mistakes in the future. Such insights are all the more relevant today because of the fears that another financial crisis could produce a similar outbreak of trade-destructive policies.

The main reason why governments resorted to import restrictions in the 1930s was that they had relatively few policy instruments with which to respond to the Great Depression. Most countries were on the gold standard and could not ease domestic monetary conditions without jeopardizing the fixed gold parity; this eliminated a monetary policy response. The economic orthodoxy of the day held that governments should respond to a downturn with austerity measures—cutting expenditures and raising taxes—to keep the budget in balance; this ruled out a fiscal policy response. Without monetary or fiscal policy as options, governments turned to trade restrictions. These measures not only failed to promote economic recovery, they made matters worse by choking off international trade.

Yet this explanation for the protectionism of the 1930s is also incomplete. A closer look at the period reveals that not all countries adopted protectionist policies to the same degree. The key to understanding which countries imposed the most protectionist measures, it turns out, is their exchange rate policy. When the Great Depression began, most countries had fixed exchange rates under the gold standard. The onset of deflation and the loss of gold reserves was the initial shock that triggered a policy response. Countries had very few ways of adjusting to this adverse development: wage and price deflation, exchange rate depreciation, or import restrictions and foreign exchange controls. Policymakers initially believed that wage and price deflation would restore equilibrium, but they gradually learned that it was failing to do so and, even worse, that it was only intensifying the contraction.

In the face of continuing deflation and loss of gold reserves, therefore, countries faced a choice between abandoning the gold standard (exchange rate depreciation) or abandoning open trade policies (protectionism). The countries that chose to remain on the gold standard and keep their exchange rate fixed still could not use monetary policy as a palliative; this pushed them toward embracing protectionism as a potential remedy. The countries that chose to abandon the gold standard and allow their currency to depreciate were freed from concerns about the balance of payments. They were able to use monetary policy to end the deflation and start the economic recovery, making it unnecessary to employ trade restrictions. Thus, the choices that countries made about their exchange rate shaped their policy response to the Great Depression. In short, the exchange rate system under the gold standard, and the constraints it imposed on policy, was intimately linked to the outbreak of protectionism in the early 1930s and destruction of the world trading system.

Chapter 1 describes the origin and spread of protectionism in the early 1930s, focusing primarily on Europe. The turning point that marked the beginning of the protectionist avalanche was not the U.S. Smoot-Hawley Tariff Act of

1930, as is often suggested, but the world financial crisis that struck in mid-1931. The financial crisis led many countries to experience balance-of-payments problems associated with gold outflows, forcing a policy response. At this point, some countries imposed exchange controls or import restrictions, both of which limited trade, to relieve pressure on the balance of payments. Other countries allowed their currencies to depreciate, which also relieved pressure on the balance of payments without the need to fall back on protectionist measures.

These events can be explained with reference to the open economy trilemma. The trilemma limits countries to choosing just two of three objectives: a fixed exchange rate, an independent monetary policy, and open trade policies. While all three objectives may be desirable, they are incompatible, and only two can be attained. Most countries wanted to have some monetary policy independence to fight deflation, but many also refused to consider any change to their gold parity. In trying to reconcile a fixed exchange rate with an independent monetary policy, these countries adopted protectionist trade measures. These countries essentially sacrificed open trade policies on the altar of the fixed exchange rate. Meanwhile, countries that allowed their currencies to depreciate generally found they no longer had balance-of-payments problems that needed to be addressed through trade restrictions.

Chapter 2 examines how different countries resolved the trilemma. Some, such as Germany, maintained the gold parity but imposed foreign exchange controls that severely limited trade and capital flows alike. Others, such as Britain, were forced off the gold standard and allowed their currencies to depreciate. Still others, such as France, remained on the gold standard and used import restrictions to compensate for their increasingly overvalued currencies. What determined which path a country followed? As the chapter explains, a country's historical experience with inflation in the 1920s played a crucial role in determining the policy choices that were made with respect to the exchange rate. Specifically, countries with a history of high inflation resisted any change to their gold parity in the belief that this would ensure monetary stability, whereas countries that did not experience high inflation over the previous decade were less concerned about the inflationary consequences of a depreciation of their currency.

Chapter 3 begins by considering how these trade restrictions contributed to the collapse of world trade. Between 1929 and 1932, the volume of world trade fell an astounding 25 percent, about half of which has been attributed to higher trade barriers. The chapter then examines empirical measures of trade policy to see if the pattern of their use is consistent with the trilemma framework. The existing data on import tariffs, import quotas, and exchange controls generally support the conclusion that countries that allowed their currencies to depreciate imposed fewer trade restrictions than those that maintained their gold parity. This finding is broadly consistent with the notion, suggested by the trilemma, that trade restrictions and exchange rate adjustments were substitutes for one another. Furthermore, these policy choices had enormous consequences for macroeconomic performance and international trade flows. When a country delinked its currency from the gold parity, it was also able to pursue a more expansionary monetary policy. At a time when prices were falling, unemployment was abnormally high, and substantial productive capacity was left unused, such policies stimulated economic growth. This enabled neighboring countries to export much more to the depreciating country than would otherwise have been the case.

Chapter 4 draws on the lessons from the trade policy experience of the 1930s to look at three issues: the relationship between the exchange rate regime and trade policy, the distinction between protectionism and mercantilism, and the reasons protectionism was not as pronounced during the recent financial crisis and recession as it was during the Great Depression.

One lesson from the 1930s is that there is a close connection between the exchange rate regime and trade policy. In particular, fixed exchange rates prevent a discretionary monetary policy response to an economic downturn; governments are required to adjust their macroeconomic policies to maintain the exchange rate rather than to ensure domestic economic stability. In addition, fixed exchange rates force governments to pay close attention to the country's balance of payments and the central bank's reserves to ensure that it is able to keep the exchange rate fixed. These features of the regime push policymakers toward using protectionist measures as an adjustment mechanism in lieu of an exchange rate change. For example, import surcharges were frequently used to help address balance-of-payments problems in the 1960s under the Bretton Woods system because exchange rate changes were discouraged.

Because of the balance-of-payments constraint that existed under the gold standard, trade policy in the 1930s was driven more by mercantilism—in the sense of limiting spending on imports to reduce the outflow of gold—than by protectionism—in the sense of sheltering import-competing producers from foreign competition. This mercantilism was not based on the erroneous confusion of gold with wealth, as Adam Smith accused earlier writers of doing, but on a simple recognition that the costs of losing gold reserves and pursuing contractionary monetary policies were extraordinarily severe. Compared to the usual description of trade policy in the 1930s, this is a very different way of viewing the developments of the period.

Finally, during the recent economic and financial crisis, the world economy largely avoided the proliferation of trade barriers that so plagued the Great Depression. There are several reasons for this difference, but an important one is that much of the world today operates under a flexible rather than a fixed exchange rate regime. Flexible exchange rates allow countries to have a monetary policy response that is unconstrained by balance-of-payments considerations and can be employed differentially across countries, depending on local conditions. Such a response should receive a great deal of credit not just for making the recession shorter than it otherwise would have been, but also for keeping protectionist pressures at bay.

This book is based on the Ohlin Lectures that I delivered at the Stockholm School of Economics on September 7–8, 2010. I am grateful to Mats Lundahl for inviting me to participate in this prestigious lecture series, which has included so many distinguished international economists. It was a privilege to pay tribute to Bertil Ohlin, who helped reshape the field of international economics. Ohlin lived through the perilous times discussed in this book and made many important contributions to the economic policy debate that raged throughout the decade (Ohlin 1931; Carlson and Jonung 2002). He had many keen insights about the relationship between exchange rate policy and trade policy that are largely consistent with the perspective presented in this book.

The invitation to give the Ohlin Lectures was particularly gratifying to me on a personal level. When I was in graduate school, I was fortunate enough to work as a research assistant to Professor Jagdish Bhagwati when he was invited to give the first Ohlin Lectures in 1987. He inaugurated the series and turned his lectures into the marvelous book *Protectionism*, published in 1988. It was a great honor to be asked to deliver the Ohlin Lectures myself twenty-three years later. The invitation also reminded me of how fortunate I was to have studied at Columbia University when it had an exceptionally strong lineup in international economics, including Jagdish Bhagwati, Ronald Findlay, and Robert Feenstra in trade, and Maurice Obstfeld, Guillermo Calvo, and Robert Mundell in finance. This book explores the connections between these two branches of international economics, which are usually considered to be separate and distinct.

I would particularly like to thank Jagdish Bhagwati and Ronald Findlay for their support and encouragement over the years. I am especially indebted to Barry Eichengreen for allowing me to draw on our joint collaboration in what follows. Two of our papers—one on the role of trade and currency blocs in altering the pattern of interwar trade (Eichengreen and Irwin 1995) and another on the reasons for protectionist trade policies during the Great Depression (Eichengreen and Irwin 2010)—deeply inform the analysis in this book. More important, he has been a role model for me and many others who have undertaken research at the intersection of international economics and economic history.

1 The Great Depression and the Rise of Protectionism

The proliferation of protectionist trade policies in the early 1930s had a lasting, adverse impact on international trade. The new barriers put a stranglehold on global commerce, contributing to a steep decline in world trade in the first half of the decade and then suppressing its growth in the second half. For these reasons, trade restrictions are commonly thought to have made the Great Depression worse and to have slowed the economic recovery. The detrimental impact of these trade barriers inspired the establishment of the General Agreement on Tariffs and Trade (GATT) after World War II.

The outbreak of protectionism was clearly a response to the Great Depression. But, as we shall see, not all countries responded in the same way. To appreciate the various reactions, we need to begin with a general understanding of why the Great Depression occurred in the first place. The specific sequence of events in the early 1930s helps explain the nature of the trade policy response to the Depression. Hence, this chapter provides some background on the causes of the Great Depression, how protectionism emerged as a result, and the reasons for the protectionist response.

The Gold Standard and the Great Depression

The world economy experienced an unprecedented catastrophe between 1929 and 1932. In almost every country, production dropped sharply and unemployment rose to historic levels. Severe price deflation put a crushing burden on debtors, which led to growing insolvency and bankruptcy. This played havoc with the financial system and reinforced the economic contraction. The Great Depression was particularly intense in the United States, where real GDP fell about 26 percent and the unemployment rate reached as high as 25 percent. Although the decline in output and the rise in unemployment were less severe elsewhere, almost no country managed to avoid a painful and prolonged economic slump during this period.[1]

Why did such a massive economic contraction strike the world at this particular moment? There is now a broad consensus among economic historians that the monetary and financial policies associated with the gold standard played a critical role in initiating and spreading the economic downturn across so many countries in such a short period of time. As countries scrambled to accumulate gold reserves, they put the world economy under growing deflationary pressure. Fixed exchange rates under the gold standard transmitted financial disturbances across countries and prevented the use of monetary policy to address the economic crisis. Recovery began only as countries peeled off from the gold standard and were able to pursue more expansionary monetary policies.

Two compelling observations support these conclusions. First, countries that were not on the gold standard managed

---

1. Romer (1993) provides a concise economic overview of the Great Depression in the United States. Kindleberger (1986) and Temin (1989) were among the first to stress the international nature of the Depression.

to avoid a deep economic slump almost entirely. For example, countries with a fiat money system (such as Spain) or those on a silver standard (such as China) did not experience a severe downturn. They suffered recessions as countries around them sank into the economic abyss but did not experience the sharp decline in industrial production or the severe deflation of prices that countries on the gold standard did.[2] Second, countries on the gold standard did not begin to recover until after they left it. A large body of research finds an association between the length and depth of a country's downturn and how long that country remained on the gold standard, as well as a strong correlation between the start of a country's recovery and when it abandoned the gold standard. As Peter Temin (1993, 92) put it, "The single best predictor of how severe the Depression was in different countries is how long they stayed on gold. The gold standard was a Midas touch that paralyzed the world economy."[3]

How was the gold standard supposed to work, and why did it fail? Under the gold standard, a country fixed the value of its currency to a certain amount of gold. By extension, this implies that the exchange rate between any two currencies on gold was also fixed. What is called the classical gold standard was established in the late nineteenth century and lasted until the outbreak of World War I in 1914. It was a stable international monetary system that had many advantages. In

2. See, for example, Choudhri and Kochin (1980), who make the comparison across exchange rate regimes. In 1934, Irving Fisher made a similar comparison and reached similar conclusions; see Dimand (2003). Grossman (1994) notes that only countries on the gold standard suffered from banking crises.
3. See, for example, Eichengreen and Sachs (1985), Temin (1989), Campa (1990), Eichengreen (1992), and Bernanke (1995). Because countries left the gold standard at different times—Britain in 1931, the United States in 1933, and France in 1936—there is sufficient variation in country experiences to identify the relationship between the decision to leave the gold standard and the start of the economic recovery.

addition to allowing the free movement of capital across countries, the system facilitated the finance of trade and promoted its expansion. Fixed exchange rates gave firms and merchants certainty about the terms on which international trade would take place and the settlement of debts and short-term credit to finance trade. As much as 20 percent of the growth in world trade between 1880 and 1910 has been attributed to the reduced uncertainty and lower transactions costs provided by the gold standard's fixed exchange rate regime.[4]

There were also disadvantages. Fixed exchange rates linked countries so closely to one another that economic and financial disturbances in one were quickly transmitted to others. In addition, because central banks were obligated to maintain the value of their currency to a certain amount of gold, the gold standard prevented the use of discretionary monetary policy. Central banks backed domestic currency and credit with their gold reserves, and a country's monetary policy was dictated by changes in its gold reserves. Under the "rules of the game," if a country had a balance-of-payments surplus and its gold holdings increased, it was supposed to accommodate the inflow by having a more inflationary monetary policy; if a country had a balance-of-payments deficit and lost gold, it was supposed to accommodate the outflow by having a more deflationary monetary policy. Thus, regardless of the state of the domestic economy, changes in gold reserves were the key factor that dictated changes in monetary policy.

Under the gold standard, this became the mechanism by which countries adjusted to economic shocks. This process was called the *price-specie flow mechanism* by David Hume,

---

4. See Lopez-Cordova and Meissner (2003). Estevadeordal, Frantz, and Taylor (2003) reach similar conclusions and also show that trade barriers were relatively stable over this period. Klein and Shambaugh (2006) find strong evidence that fixed exchange rates promote trade today.

who described its operation in 1752 in his famous essay, "Of Money." For example, if a country began to run a large trade deficit, either because of a growing demand for imports or because of falling demand for its exports, the excess imports would have to be financed by an outflow of gold. The outflow of gold would cause a monetary contraction that would tend to reduce domestic wages and prices. As a result, the country's exports would become less expensive on world markets and foreign goods would become more expensive in its domestic market. This change in prices would reduce the trade deficit by stimulating exports and discouraging imports. Meanwhile, countries that were gaining gold would have to pursue an expansionary monetary policy, which would lead to higher wages and prices in those countries. This would make their exports less competitive and increase their imports from others, reducing their trade surpluses. This process would automatically help restore equilibrium to the balance of payments.

Without discretionary authority over monetary policy, however, governments lacked an important instrument that might have cushioned any adverse economic shocks coming from other countries and transmitted through the gold standard. Because a country's monetary policy was influenced by gold inflows and outflows, a country on the gold standard might not be able to ensure domestic price stability. Furthermore, the burden of adjustment fell on changing domestic wages and prices rather than on changing just one price— the exchange rate. Still, the classical gold standard of the late nineteenth century is generally believed to have functioned well, in part because wages and prices were flexible.

Although most countries suspended the gold standard during World War I, they planned to return to it sometime after the war. When peace came, however, many countries had difficulty reestablishing stable monetary conditions, a necessary condition for a return to the gold standard. Germany suffered a devastating hyperinflation in 1922–1923, and many Central European countries, including Austria, Hungary, and Poland, also endured a period of severe inflation. In addition, France, Belgium, and others experienced a traumatic bout of high inflation in 1924–1926. This monetary turbulence led to political conflict and social unrest. These problems not only delayed the reestablishment of the gold standard, they left countries deeply averse to monetary instability and profoundly afraid of inflation.[5]

By the end of the decade, most countries had got their monetary situation under control and were able to rejoin the gold standard. Unfortunately, problems with the newly reconstructed gold standard quickly emerged.

First, Britain and France reestablished gold parities at misaligned rates. In 1925, Britain restored the convertibility of the pound at its old prewar parity even though domestic prices had risen during the war but had not yet returned to prewar levels. As a result, the pound was overvalued, which made British goods expensive on the world market and foreign goods inexpensive in its domestic market. This led to trade deficits and balance-of-payments problems, forcing the Bank of England to maintain a tight monetary policy in an effort to retain existing gold reserves. Officials hoped that this tight policy stance would deflate domestic wages and prices enough to restore the balance-of-payments to equilibrium. In fact, high interest rates discouraged investment and kept unemployment

---

5. Reflecting this traumatic experience, John Maynard Keynes (1919) wrote in *The Economic Consequences of the Peace*: "Lenin is said to have declared that the best way to destroy the Capitalistic System was to debauch the currency. . . . Lenin was certainly right. There is no subtler, no surer means of overturning the existing basis of society than to debauch the currency. The process engages all the hidden forces of economic law on the side of destruction."

high because workers resisted any cut in wages. Labor unrest grew, and in 1926 there was a violent general strike. Meanwhile, the French franc was restored to convertibility at a rate much lower than its prewar parity. The undervaluation more than compensated for the rise in its price level and gave France balance-of-payments surpluses that led to the accumulation of an enormous stockpile of gold reserves. France's share of world gold reserves rose from 7 percent in 1926 to 27 percent in 1932.[6] As France drained gold from the rest of the world, other countries were forced to pursue more restrictive monetary policies.

A second problem with the reconstructed gold standard was the lack of any formal agreement about the conduct of monetary policy. Under the classical gold standard, shifts in gold reserves were supposed to elicit symmetric responses: countries losing gold would deflate while countries gaining gold would inflate their money supplies. These were the so-called "rules of the game." But in the interwar period, the price-specie flow mechanism was not allowed to work. Two key countries, the United States and France, violated the rules by preventing gold inflows from leading to a domestic monetary expansion; in other words, they sterilized gold inflows. This asymmetry created a deflationary bias: while countries losing gold reserves would be forced to deflate, countries gaining gold reserves did not necessarily inflate. The burden of adjustment was also asymmetric: countries with a balance-of-payments deficit were forced to change their policy because their dwindling gold reserves were finite, but countries with a surplus did not have to change any of their policies and could continue accumulating reserves indefinitely.

War debts and reparations were a third cause of postwar instability. The postwar settlement required Germany to

---

6. See Johnson (1997), Mouré (2002), and Irwin (2010a).

make reparation payments to Britain and France, which in turn were required to repay war loans from the United States. The system worked reasonably well in the mid-1920s because U.S. capital markets engaged in large-scale foreign lending to Germany. These capital flows were recycled to Britain and France and then worked their way back to the United States. As long as the United States continued to be a creditor to the world, the flow of funds smoothed the repayment of debts around the world. However, if the stream of American lending dried up, the whole international financial system would be seriously disrupted.

The problems with the newly reconstituted gold standard began to emerge in 1928, when the Federal Reserve tightened monetary policy in response to the booming stock market. As interest rates rose, the United States curtailed its foreign lending and attracted gold from other countries (Hamilton 1987; Eichengreen 1992). Because the United States was sterilizing its gold inflows, they did not affect the monetary base or money supply. This constituted a deflationary shock from the standpoint of the rest of the world, which was losing gold and had to tighten monetary policy without the benefit of a more expansionary U.S. policy.

Meanwhile, France was reinforcing the deflationary impact on the rest of the world. The undervaluation of the franc led to trade surpluses that produced large gold inflows. In addition, the Bank of France decided to exchange its holdings of British pounds and other currencies for gold from other central banks. These policies allowed France to accumulate an enormous stockpile of gold reserves, and, as we have seen, its share of world gold reserves soared. France also prevented the monetization of its gold inflows so that, despite the large increase in its gold reserves, the nation's money supply did not increase.

The violation of the gold standard rules by the United States and France set the stage for worldwide deflation. According to one estimate, between 1928 and 1930, the United States and France took 11 percent of the world's gold stock away from other countries and effectively demonetized it (Irwin 2010b). Not surprisingly, starting in mid-1929, wholesale prices around the world began to decline sharply. This large, unanticipated deflation continued unabated until about 1933.

This cartoon by David Low, published in the *Evening Standard* on September 19, 1931, shows the United States and France draining gold from the rest of the world and putting it in a reservoir where it would be left unused. Meanwhile, the rest of the world is left to flounder in the pool of diminishing reserves. *Source*: British Cartoon Archive, University of Kent. Reproduced with permission from Associated Newspapers Ltd./Solo Syndication.

By one measure, world commodity prices fell 34 percent between 1928 and 1932. The deflation proved enormously destructive. When prices fell, producers could stay profitable only by reducing their costs. Because workers resisted wage reductions, firms could cut costs only by reducing output and laying off workers. With their cash flow reduced, firms and households also found it more difficult to service their debts, which were fixed in nominal terms. As a result, nonperforming loans increased. Growing insolvency and bankruptcy made banks reluctant to lend to borrowers whose creditworthiness was uncertain. The deterioration in bank balance sheets made them susceptible to bank runs, which caused banks to further reduce lending so that they could increase their holdings of emergency reserves. All of these factors reinforced one another and intensified the economic contraction. Around the world, output fell and unemployment rose.

Most countries tolerated deflation year after year because they believed it was a temporary phenomenon that would eventually restore equilibrium. The strategy might have been successful if some countries had been experiencing deflation and others inflation, but with all countries caught in a deflationary cycle, it did not work. As the slump deepened, the monetary retrenchment could continue for only so long before democratically elected governments would begin to face the electoral consequences. Yet most countries endured economic hardship much longer than would be thought reasonable today because of the strong hold of the gold standard on the minds of government officials and the public, something Eichengreen and Temin (2000) have called the "gold standard mentality."

Did any of the world's leading economists understand the flaws in the interwar gold standard and anticipate the cascade of events that produced such a great deflation? The Swedish economist Gustav Cassel was among the most prescient. He had long worried about a worldwide shortage of gold after World War I and insisted that international cooperation would be needed to maintain a well-functioning gold standard. Cassel expressed alarm about the dangers of too many central banks trying to acquire gold reserves at the same time. If central bank demand for gold holdings outstripped the slowly growing supply of gold, the price of gold would normally rise. But because the nominal price of gold was fixed in terms of domestic currency, it could not rise. Instead, the price of all other goods would have to fall, causing a generalized deflation of prices.

Lecturing at Columbia University in 1928, prior to the onset of the worldwide deflation, Cassel warned that

the great problem before us is how to meet the growing scarcity of gold which threatens the world both from increased demand and from diminished supply. We must solve the problem by a systematic restriction of the monetary demand for gold. Only if we succeed in doing this can we hope to prevent a permanent fall of the general price level and a prolonged and worldwide depression which would inevitably be connected with such a fall in prices. (Cassel 1928, 44)

He correctly predicted that the intensity of the deflationary pressure would lead to a depression and the eventual abandonment of the gold standard:

The absolute necessity of international cooperation on broad lines for the stabilization of the value of gold is most clearly seen if we only for a moment reflect on the alternative to such cooperation. This would obviously be a general and ruthless competition for gold, a consequent continual rise in the value of gold [and decline in prices of all other goods], and a corresponding, world-wide economic depression for an unlimited future. A very disagreeable consequence of such a movement in the value of gold would be a general aggravation of all debts contracted in a gold standard, doubtless in many cases followed by an incapacity to pay debts or a refusal to do so. We must remember that the great part of the world that would have to suffer from such a development has a very powerful weapon of defense. This weapon is simply the abolition of gold as a monetary standard. (Cassel 1928, 99)

The deflationary problem that Cassel outlined could have been avoided in several ways. The United States and France could have played by the rules of the game and stopped sterilizing their gold inflows. Alternatively, if all countries wanted to hold more gold reserves, they could have agreed to raise simultaneously the nominal price at which they pegged their currency to gold—that is, the price of gold could have been revalued. This would have preserved existing bilateral exchange rates but would have given countries the monetary breathing space to avoid the costly deflation of the period. Another option would have been to reach an international agreement to allow countries losing gold reserves and suffering most from deflation to devalue their currencies against gold.

But Cassel's call for international cooperation went unheeded because some countries, such as France, were perfectly satisfied with the status quo and did not see the need to change anything.[7] Unfortunately, his predictions came true, worldwide deflation and depression were the result, and the consequences were catastrophic. In his Nobel Prize lecture, Robert Mundell (2000, 331) speculated that "had the price of gold been raised in the late 1920's, or, alternatively, had the major central banks pursued policies of price stability instead of adhering to the gold standard, there would have been no Great Depression, no Nazi revolution, and no World War II."

---

7. The League of Nations opened an inquiry into the gold problem, but central banks were reluctant to cooperate, and the final report was ignored. See Clavin and Wessels (2004).

Moving toward Protectionism: The Smoot-Hawley Tariff

To this point, we have discussed the international monetary system without any mention of the international trading system. Their interrelationship will soon become evident. But first we must ask, what was the world's trade policy situation in the 1920s, and did the United States, as is commonly thought, initiate the spread of protectionist policies around the world by enacting the Smoot-Hawley tariff in 1930?

Prior to World War I, import duties were the most frequently used trade restriction employed by governments. There were no multilateral trade agreements, such as the GATT, that capped a country's tariff level, but the world's major economies were linked together through a series of bilateral trade agreements. These agreements included the unconditional most-favored-nation (MFN) clause, ensuring that each would grant nondiscriminatory tariff treatment to one another. However, during the war, countries imposed not only higher tariffs but a host of other trade restrictions as well, including import quotas, export and import licenses, and exchange controls. In the early 1920s, these administrative controls were phased out slowly, although tariff levels were often adjusted upward to offset the removal of the other restrictions.[8]

By the mid-1920s, the worldwide monetary situation had stabilized and countries began tentative efforts to reduce trade barriers. As countries concluded new commercial agreements, the MFN clause was resurrected and with it the

---

8. A League of Nations (1927) study found that tariff levels were higher in 1925 than they had been in 1913. For a general discussion of this period, see Marrison (2000).

provisions for nondiscriminatory tariff treatment. Countries also began to discuss a coordinated reduction in trade barriers. The 1927 World Economic Conference, sponsored by the League of Nations, called for multilateral negotiations to scale back tariff and non-tariff barriers to world trade. Although such negotiations were not imminent, government officials seemed to believe that progress was being made toward this goal. Many countries appeared willing to sign the Convention for the Abolition of Import and Export Prohibitions and Restrictions and prepare for negotiations that would reduce import tariffs.

Unfortunately, this nascent movement toward trade liberalization was cut short. The onset of a worldwide recession in 1929 gave governments a reason to postpone any efforts to dismantle trade barriers. But the decision by the United States to enact the Smoot-Hawley tariff in June 1930 is often singled out and blamed for starting the movement toward higher trade barriers. The United States was the first major country to increase its import duties around this time, and other countries seemed to follow its lead. However, while there is no doubt that the Smoot-Hawley tariff was a harmful development, it was not the primary cause of the worldwide movement toward protectionism during the Great Depression.

The Smoot-Hawley tariff was first conceived in late 1928 as part of an election ploy by Republicans to gain the farm vote.[9] Its original purpose was to help financially distressed farmers cope with low agricultural prices. Unfortunately, because most American farmers depended on export markets, higher tariffs on imports did nothing to improve their situation. And once Congress started increasing agricultural duties, the

---

9. For a recent overview of the Smoot-Hawley tariff, see Irwin (2011).

process got carried away, and many duties on manufactured products were also increased.[10]

The increase in U.S. import duties was not a response to the Depression. The decision to increase tariffs had been made in 1928 when the economy was strong. The duties in the bill were largely set when the House of Representatives passed it in May 1929, several months before the U.S. business cycle peak in August and the stock market crash in October. Because of delays in the Senate, the measure was not finalized and signed into law until June 1930. By this time, the United States was in a recession, but its severity was far from evident.

The Smoot-Hawley tariff was a large but not a massive shock to U.S. imports, and to world trade more generally. First, trade was a small part of the overall U.S. economy; about two-thirds of U.S. imports were duty-free, and dutiable imports were just 1.4 percent of GDP in 1929. Second, the increase in tariff rates was large but not astronomical. The Smoot-Hawley legislation raised the average tariff on dutiable imports from about 38 percent to 45 percent, an increase in rates of about six percentage points, or 20 percent, which was only enough to increase the average price of dutiable

---

10. American economists voiced strong objections to the tariff bill at the time. A statement signed by 1,028 American economists called the higher tariffs "a mistake" and urged Congress to reject or the president to veto the measure. They pointed out that protection was unnecessary because most producers were not suffering as a result of foreign competition. Furthermore, exports would suffer because "countries cannot permanently buy from us unless they are permitted to sell to us, and the more we restrict importation of goods from them by means of even higher tariffs, the more we reduce the possibility of exporting to them." Finally, higher tariffs would "inevitably inject . . . bitterness" into international economic relations and, by violating the spirit of the League of Nations' World Economic Conference of 1927, "plainly invite other nations to compete with us in raising further barriers to trade." See Irwin (2011, 222–225).

imports by about 5 percent. Still, the tariff was significant enough to slash dutiable imports by about 15 percent and cut total imports by about 5 percent.

From the perspective of other countries, only 6 percent of Europe's exports were destined for the U.S. market. European manufactured goods were particularly affected by the higher tariffs, although declining U.S. demand for imported goods, a consequence of the recession, was a far greater problem for most foreign exporters. The recession helped reduce the volume of imports by 15 percent in the year prior to the imposition of the Smoot-Hawley tariff, a period when U.S. real GDP fell 7 percent.

The Smoot-Hawley tariff was not a major factor in causing the Great Depression. Given the overriding importance of monetary and financial factors in bringing about the Depression, the tariff almost certainly played a small role, if any, in the economic debacle. At a time when dutiable imports were just 1.4 percent of GDP, a 5 percent increase in the price of dutiable imports could not have triggered an economic downturn of great magnitude. In fact, economists across the spectrum have been skeptical about blaming Smoot-Hawley for the severity of the Great Depression.[11] The economic decline was already well underway when the legislation was enacted.

Most important for our purposes, the Smoot-Hawley tariff did not trigger a worldwide trade war. Many believe that the Smoot-Hawley tariff initiated the movement toward higher

---

11. As Temin (1989, 46) notes: "The idea that the Smoot-Hawley tariff was a major cause of the Depression is an enduring conviction . . . . Despite its popularity, however, this argument fails on both theoretical and historical grounds." For example, the United States had increased or decreased the import duties by greater amounts in the past without it having led to a macroeconomic disaster; see Irwin (2011) for more details.

import duties simply because it came first. This is contra-
dicted by a 1931 League of Nations report on trade policy
developments between 1929 and mid-1931. The report be-
moaned the growth in agricultural trade barriers, but the
changes in world trade policies it noted were mild compared
to what was to come. Indeed, the League (1942b, 136) later
conceded that Smoot-Hawley's "direct effect on the course of
world policy in the years that followed became of secondary
importance" as the Depression deepened.

At the same time, other countries deeply resented the
American tariff hike and protested against it. Although only
6 percent of Europe's exports were destined for the U.S. market, those exports earned critical dollars that could be used
to repay loans and finance imports. European nations were
angry that the world's largest creditor nation, after having
already increased tariffs significantly in 1922, was creating
additional obstacles for countries that were still struggling to
pay off their World War I debts. The United States had failed
to join the League of Nations and now appeared to undermine efforts to coordinate a tariff truce that promised to stop
any movement toward greater protectionism. Moreover, the
United States was in a deepening recession that threatened to
bring the rest of the world down with it.

This resentment led to retaliation against the United States.
Canada, America's largest trading partner, suffered the most
from the higher tariff. Shortly before the duties took effect,
Canada responded by imposing higher tariffs on certain U.S.
goods and by increasing the margin of preference given to
British goods. This was not enough to satisfy the outraged
Canadian electorate. The Smoot-Hawley tariff contributed to
the electoral defeat of the pro-American Liberal government
in July 1930 and the election of the pro-British Conservative
Party. The Conservatives retaliated by imposing even higher

duties on U.S. goods and proposed a preferential trade agreement with Britain (McDonald, O'Brien, and Callahan 1997). Other countries also retaliated specifically against the United States, by levying higher duties on automobiles, for example, but there was no worldwide trade war. While it played a modest role in the spread of protectionism and the collapse of world trade in the early 1930s, the Smoot-Hawley tariff contributed more directly to the rise of an especially damaging development, the spread of discriminatory trade policies. Such policies encourage trade with selected countries by lowering duties on goods from favored countries or raising duties on goods from non-favored countries. These trade preferences divert trade more than they destroy it; that is, they shift trade flows between countries to a much greater extent than nondiscriminatory trade policies. For example, if a country increased its tariffs uniformly against all imports, U.S. exports would likely decline in roughly the same proportion as other exports to that market, and the United States would maintain its share of a smaller market. However, if there were even a slight amount of discrimination against American goods in favor of other suppliers, U.S. exporters could lose the entire market.

The most significant discriminatory trade arrangement of the period was the system of imperial preferences established by Britain and its former colonies at a conference in Ottawa, Canada, in 1932. At this conference, these countries agreed to reduce tariffs on each other's goods in an effort to promote intrabloc trade. Although imperial preferences were not established in direct retaliation against the United States, the international climate against the Smoot-Hawley tariff helped give rise to it. "Unquestionably the American Congress had precipitated the tariff responses in both Canada and the United Kingdom," Kottman (1968, 37) notes. "Shortly before the Ottawa Conference, the American chargé in the Canadian capital reported a 'quiet but definite undercurrent of antagonism and bitterness towards the United States trade policy' whenever comments were made of the impending gathering."[12]

Resentment against the United States made it a particular target of those discriminatory policies. U.S. exports particularly suffered in two of its major markets, Britain and Canada. The U.S. share of world exports fell from 15.6 percent in 1929 to 12.4 percent in 1932, partly as a result of this discrimination. The United States spent the better part of the next two decades trying to dismantle the discriminatory trade bloc created by imperial preferences that put U.S. exporters at such a competitive disadvantage in major foreign markets.

In sum, the Smoot-Hawley tariff was harmful and unnecessary and led to retaliation and discrimination against the United States. It may have contributed to the growth of protectionist sentiment in other countries, but it did not spark a worldwide trade war that destroyed the world trading system. That happened almost exactly a year after the Smoot-Hawley tariff was imposed, and it was the result of a different chain of events.

Things Fall Apart—1931

The series of unfortunate events that undermined the world trading system began with the European financial crisis in

---

12. Furthermore, this official noted, "most of the people I have talked to have not failed to refer to our tariff and to accuse it of starting the world movement toward restriction of trade." Indeed, the Conservative prime minister defended the Ottawa agreements before Parliament by stating that the country needed an advantage in exporting to the United Kingdom over the United States to make up for the lost markets in the United States as a result of the Smoot-Hawley tariff.

mid-1931. In May 1931, Austria's largest bank, Credit Anstalt, failed. This failure contributed to a financial panic that spread to neighboring countries and the rest of the world and ultimately destroyed the gold standard. The world trading system was brought down along with it. The collapse of Credit Anstalt was also intertwined with the trade politics of the day and illustrates why international economic cooperation was so difficult in the interwar period.

In March 1931, Austria and Germany revealed plans to establish a customs union. This news was greeted with fierce protests by France and Czechoslovakia. They feared that the venture marked a return of German expansionism and claimed that it violated Germany's treaty obligations. Weeks later, a bank run on Credit Anstalt turned into a massive flight from the schilling, and Austria desperately sought emergency funding to prevent a financial collapse. As a condition for financial assistance, France insisted that the planned customs union be dropped. France exploited the situation by withdrawing funds from Austria, putting it under additional financial pressure and thereby weakening its position.[13] Austria was soon forced to capitulate, and it agreed to drop the customs union in exchange for an international loan package.

When the Credit Anstalt crisis occurred, two years of continuous deflation had already weakened banking systems around the world. As a result of the crisis, investors became even more nervous about potential fragilities in the world's financial system. The Austrian crisis was quickly followed by banking and currency crises in Germany, where depositors

---

13. As Aguado (2001, 214) put it: "The French were not only demanding political concessions in exchange for the funds necessary to avoid a banking moratorium, but were actually withdrawing funds from Austria in order to accentuate the flight from schilling which made the Austrian government dependent on foreign help in the first place."

began massive withdrawals of funds from the banking system and demanded gold in exchange for marks.[14] Germany's government depended on foreign loans to finance its expenditures, and the loss of those loans, partly as a result of the customs union dispute, triggered a run on the mark and the loss of gold reserves. In July, with its gold reserves rapidly disappearing, Germany imposed strict controls on all foreign exchange transactions to prevent further losses. While Germany officially maintained the gold parity of the reichsmark, the country effectively went off the gold standard because the mark was no longer freely convertible into gold. The government essentially took control of all the foreign exchange earned by exporters and began to ration it among importers. Just days after Germany imposed exchange controls, Hungary and Chile followed suit to prevent the loss of their gold and foreign exchange reserves.

Financial pressure then spread to Britain, whose balance-of-payments position had been weak for some time. British banks were large creditors to Germany and Austria, and now their financial health seemed questionable. An official report in July also suggested that the government's fiscal deficit was much larger than expected. Following this, investors began selling pound-denominated assets, and in August and September 1931, the Bank of England lost enormous sums of gold. Interest rate hikes failed to support the currency because confidence could not be so easily bought. With its gold reserves declining at an accelerating rate, Britain relented to the financial pressure and, on September 21, 1931, it abandoned the gold standard. Being an international

---

14. The German crisis appears to have been independent of the Austrian crisis, although there may have been some spillover effect in making investors nervous about the security of their investments; see chapter 2 and Temin (2008).

financial center, Britain did not opt for exchange controls as Germany did. Rather, the Bank of England simply allowed the pound to depreciate against other currencies on the foreign exchange market. Within weeks, the currency had fallen about 30 percent against the U.S. dollar and other currencies that remained on gold.

Other countries with important trade and financial links to Britain also experienced gold losses. About eighteen of them quickly followed Britain in leaving the gold standard and allowing their currencies to depreciate. These countries included Denmark, Finland, Norway, Sweden, Portugal, Egypt, Bolivia, and Latvia. Japan followed in December 1931, Greece in April 1932, and Thailand and Peru in May 1932.

Britain's decision to float the pound put financial pressure on countries that remained on the gold standard. The United States was next as market participants sold dollars and demanded gold in return; the Federal Reserve lost 15 percent of its gold reserves in the month following the British action. At a time when the United States was already deeply mired in the Depression, the Federal Reserve Bank of New York raised its discount rate from 1.5 percent to 3.5 percent to fend off the attack (Hamilton 1988). This decision demonstrated that maintaining the exchange rate parity was a more important objective to the Federal Reserve than aiding the domestic economy, which was still mired in a severe slump.[15] Higher interest rates choked domestic investment even further and plunged the economy into the abyss. In fact, this tightening of monetary policy in late 1931 was a key factor that turned a deep recession into the Great Depression. Although the

---

15. The decision to raise interest rates also came in response to a French threat to exchange dollars for gold. Having been burned by the British decision to allow the pound to depreciate, France did not want to see its dollar holdings similarly sink in value.

United States' abundant gold reserves and the interest rate hike soon restored confidence in the dollar and eased the pressure on the Federal Reserve, the damage was done. Other countries managed to escape the global financial turmoil of 1931 relatively unscathed. With its large stock of gold reserves, France's commitment to the gold standard was unquestioned. In fact, during the 1931 crisis, there was a flight to the franc and the country's gold reserves increased. In addition, Belgium, the Netherlands, and Switzerland remained on the gold standard without much difficulty.

However, after Britain and the others allowed their currencies to depreciate, the currencies of countries that remained on the gold standard were now overvalued relative to those no longer linked to gold. Over time, this led to a deterioration in their trade balances, as their exports became more expensive for foreign consumers and imports from abroad became cheaper. The countries that remained on the gold standard faced the problem of how, at the new configuration of exchange rates, to bring their high domestic costs of production in line with the lower costs abroad. This in turn put pressure on the balance of payments, and they gradually began to lose gold, putting them in a slow deflationary squeeze.

Trade Policy Reaction

The year 1931 marked a turning point in the Great Depression. In countries that followed Britain off the gold standard, the primary objective of monetary policy was no longer maintaining the fixed exchange rate through the gold parity. They were now free to pursue more expansionary monetary policies, allowing them to reduce interest rates, end the deflation, and stabilize their financial systems—all of which permitted the economic recovery to begin. However, countries that remained on the gold standard now suffered from overvalued currencies and had to maintain high interest rates to retain their gold reserves and keep the exchange rate fixed. In these countries, the economic slump continued. But the British decision to abandon the gold standard and allow the pound to depreciate also had enormous consequences for trade policy. First, the decision made investors even more nervous about the commitment of other countries to the gold standard. This led to a scramble to exchange currency for gold in countries whose commitment to the gold standard was now brought into question. As these countries lost gold reserves, many chose to impose exchange controls to prevent capital flight. During September and October 1931, exchange controls were introduced or tightened in Uruguay, Colombia, Greece, Czechoslovakia, Iceland, Bolivia, Yugoslavia, Austria, Argentina, Norway, and Denmark (Gordon 1941, 54–55). Exchange controls gave government authorities the ability to control and allocate all foreign exchange earnings. They were used not only to prevent the export of gold but also to reduce spending on imports. As we shall see, exchange controls became the most restrictive trade practices of the 1930s.

Second, the depreciation of the pound, and the other currencies linked to it, was so large and sharp that it dramatically changed competitive conditions in world trade overnight. The depreciation of the pound made the price of British and sterling-priced goods significantly less expensive on world markets. The improved competitive position of exports from countries with depreciated currencies prompted countermeasures from countries that remained on the gold standard and now suffered from overvalued currencies. Within weeks, these countries ratcheted up their tariffs to block cheap imports from countries whose currencies had fallen in value.

A month after the pound depreciated, France imposed a 15 percent surcharge on goods from Britain and more than a dozen other countries to offset the depreciation of sterling. It also began a system of restrictive import quotas to limit spending on foreign goods. In January 1932, the German government began to raise "equalizing" tariffs on goods that came from countries with depreciated currencies. In early 1932 the Netherlands, which traditionally had a policy of free trade, increased duties by 25 percent, partly to offset the competitive advantage gained by sterling area producers. Canada and South Africa, which remained on the gold standard despite their close economic ties to Britain, imposed antidumping duties aimed at cheap imports from Britain. In the United States, Congress considered, but did not act upon, proposals to levy countervailing duties on imports from countries with depreciated currencies.

In short, when Britain went off the gold standard, a chaotic scramble to restrict trade and close markets began. Countries that did not follow Britain either imposed exchange controls to protect existing gold reserves against speculative attack or imposed tariffs and quotas to protect domestic markets from cheap imports, or did both. As some countries raised trade barriers, other countries objected and retaliated, particularly if the move to restrict imports was accomplished by administrative actions (either import quotas or exchange controls) that were perceived to be discriminatory and unfair. This led to a bad dynamic in which trade restrictions begat more trade restrictions, leading to a sharp plunge in world trade in late 1931 and early 1932.

This mushrooming of restrictions had dire consequences for world trade and the payments system. The League of Nations' *World Economic Survey 1931/32* described the fallout:

It is impossible in any brief summary to make anything like a complete statement of all the various devices brought into use to restrict trade. Especially after the abandonment of the gold standard by Great Britain in September 1931, there has been a veritable panic, which has piled new tariffs on old, turned licensing systems into prohibitions, monopolies and contingents; denounced existing commercial agreements; created more and more rigid exchange controls issuing in debt moratoria and paralysing trade; and substituted a slight and temporary framework of clearing agreements for previous existing treaties. The bankers or civil servants had had thrust on them the duty of regulating commercial intercourse, and merchants have been so hemmed in by regulations that freedom of trade has almost ceased to exist. . . . There has never before been such a wholesale and widespread retreat from international economic cooperation. (League of Nations 1932, 289–290)

The next year's *Survey* again recounted the dramatic events set in motion by Britain's decision to abandon gold:

The multiplicity and variety of these emergency restrictions [on international trade] after September 1931 is difficult to summarise in a few words. . . . In the sixteen months after September 1st, 1931, general tariff increases had been imposed in twenty-three countries, in three of them twice during the period—with only one case of a general tariff reduction. Customs duties had been increased on individual items or groups of commodities by fifty countries, in most cases by a succession of enactments which, in several countries, numbers over twenty tariff changes in the sixteen months. Import quotas, prohibitions, licensing systems and similar quantitative restrictions, with even more frequent changes in several important cases, had been imposed by thirty-two countries. . . . This bare list is utterly inadequate to portray the harassing complexity of the emergency restrictions that were superimposed upon an already fettered world trade after the period of exchange instability was inaugurated by the abandonment of the gold standard by the United Kingdom in September 1931. By the middle of 1932, it was obvious that the international trading mechanism was in real danger of being smashed as completely as the international monetary system had been. (League of Nations 1933, 16–17)

The primary goal of this protectionism was to strengthen the balance of payments—reduce imports, improve the trade balance, and stop gold outflows—by any measure possible. Policies included both the traditional measure of import tariffs and the so-called "new protectionism," consisting of import quotas, import licenses, export subsidies, and exchange controls, which had rarely been used during peacetime.[16] These different policy measures deserve some elaboration.

The higher tariffs of the period ranged from general tariff revisions to selective countervailing or antidumping duties aimed at countries with depreciated currencies. As the League of Nations (1933, 193–194) put it:

When currency instability on a wide scale was unloosed after the United Kingdom abandoned the gold standard in September 1931, tariff increases, like other restrictions on trade, began to follow one another in the most rapid succession. During 1932, there were general tariff increases in the United Kingdom, Egypt, Norway, Japan, Portugal, Greece, Siam, South Africa, Australia, Belgium, Latvia, the Netherlands, the Dutch East Indies, Nicaragua, Persia, and Venezuela. Partial increases, repeated several times in most cases, were recorded in practically every country for which information is available.

In order to increase import duties, some countries had to violate commercial agreements in which they had agreed to

---

16. The League of Nations (1933, 196–197) elaborated by noting that the "rapid adoption in a large number of countries of emergency measures of trade restriction aimed primarily at direct quantitative limitation of imports, and in some cases of exports. This new protectionism has not taken the place of higher tariffs—import duties . . . are now higher and more flexible than ever. But it has effectively supplemented and completed their restrictive effects. Administrative measures, such as prohibitions, quotas, licensing systems and clearing agreements, have never before been used as a general method of trade regulation except in the altogether abnormal circumstances of the war and immediate post-war years." Kindleberger (1989) provides a descriptive overview of commercial policy during this period.

bind their tariffs at existing levels. Renouncing or not renew-
ing commercial treaties and agreements generated friction
between countries and led to reprisals and counter-reprisals.
For example, when France abrogated the Franco-Germany
commercial agreement, Germany imposed restrictions on
agricultural imports from France. Then France responded by
tightening quotas on goods imported from Germany. Such tit-
for-tat retaliations occurred frequently starting in late 1931.

Some countries, such as France, did not directly violate
existing commercial agreements but rather broke the spirit
of such agreements by imposing quantitative restrictions on

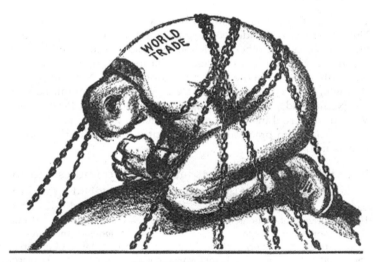

Tariff Shackles
—Fitzpatrick in the St. Louis "Post-Dispatch."

This May 1931 cartoon by Daniel Fitzpatrick of the *St. Louis Post Dispatch*
shows world trade shackled by tariff chains. *Source*: State Historical Society
of Missouri. Reproduced with permission.

imports. Quotas were overlooked in most commercial agree-ments, and hence employing them was not a formal violation. Although import quotas were similar to tariffs in reducing trade, they distorted markets even more. The quantity of imports was rigidly fixed and could not adjust to changing demand conditions. In addition, the quotas required gov-ernment bureaucrats to allocate the fixed quantities across different suppliers, often arbitrarily and without regard to economic efficiency.

Exchange controls were perhaps the most draconian trade policy measure used during this period (Ohlin 1937). Ex-change controls allowed a nation's central bank to impound all the foreign exchange earnings of the country's exporters and to allocate it to selected importers for the purchase of goods from abroad. In essence, exchange controls enabled a government to control all payments to foreigners, whether to import a good, repay a debt, or for any other purpose. The goal was to limit spending on imports, put a stop to capi-tal flight and the external drain on reserves, and allow the country to maintain its gold parity. Government authori-ties could ration the foreign exchange to limit spending on imports, or otherwise allocate the funds to serve whatever purposes it wished. While exchange controls were rarely completely effective, the League of Nations (1933, 198) noted that the existence of such controls in so many countries was "a powerful factor in compressing the total quantities and values of imports and therefore of exports." In addition, ex-change controls required an army of government bureaucrats to evaluate and process all the competing claims for foreign exchange.

As exchange controls began disrupting the international payments system, governments started to conserve their for-eign exchange reserves by engaging in negotiated bilateral trade deals. Government-brokered bulk-trading arrangements began to displace commercial transactions between private entities in world trade. For example, in 1932 a state deal was made to exchange 29,000 Hungarian pigs for 20,000 wagons of Czech wood fuel (League of Nations 1933, 200). Brazil banned the import of wheat by private merchants so that the government could negotiate deals to export coffee in exchange for wheat. An Anglo-Danish treaty in 1933 guaranteed that Britain would import a certain amount of bacon from Denmark, and in return Denmark would import a certain amount of British coal. In many cases, the problems in international finance and the disruptions to the multilateral payments system reduced international trade to barter.

Even countries that did not adopt exchange controls had other ways of exerting control over imports and conserving on foreign exchange. State trading monopolies, import monopolies of particular products, import licenses, export licenses, export quotas, and export subsidies were among the multitude of trade interventions practiced during the 1930s. Countries put in place a complex system of trade regulation that went far beyond the old method of just using tariffs to limit imports. Because most of these policies gave government authorities the discretion to allocate import quotas or foreign exchange, the nondiscriminatory intention of the MFN clause was lost. The 1927 World Economic Conference's goal of reducing trade barriers and restoring the unconditional MFN clause was completely shattered.

Thus, the European financial crisis of mid-1931, which drove a significant group of countries off the gold standard, led to chaos in the international trading system. The financial crisis and its consequences bear much more of the responsibility for the worldwide deterioration in trade policy than the Smoot-Hawley tariff. As Hubert Henderson (1955,

By Fitzpatrick, in the St. Louis *Post-Dispatch*
THE FOUR HORSEMEN OF THE WORLD TRADE SLUMP

This July 1932 cartoon by Daniel Fitzpatrick of the *St. Louis Post Dispatch* shows the four horsemen of the world trade slump: war, tariff, debts and reparations, and scarcity of gold. *Source*: State Historical Society of Missouri. Reproduced with permission.

250), an economist with the Economic Advisory Council in Britain, later wrote, "it is improbable in the extreme that the international monetary breakdown [in 1931] could have been avoided, or that the subsequent story would have been materially different, if the American tariff had been left unchanged."

The trade restrictions that suddenly appeared in late 1931 were not, for the most part, imposed because of special interest lobbying. By that time, the world economy had been in a serious recession for about two years. If trade-affected special interests, either industrial or agricultural, were going to lobby governments for protectionist trade policies, they would already have done so. Furthermore, because of the deepening recession, import penetration was actually falling; foreign competition was less of a factor for many industries because trade was collapsing faster than production. This is not to say that special interests played no role in the increase in trade barriers. Even if import penetration was falling, foreign goods were still blamed for low prices, and hence there were still frequent calls for tariff hikes to protect the domestic market from those falling prices, particularly for agricultural goods. But special interests were a secondary factor in explaining the sudden and dramatic increase in trade barriers in the last quarter of 1931.

Instead of protecting import-competing domestic producers from foreign competition, the main purpose of the trade restrictions was to protect gold reserves and strengthen the balance of payments. By reducing imports, governments hoped they could improve the balance of trade and thereby stabilize or increase the country's gold reserves. The initial restrictions on trade and payments materialized very quickly; they were emergency measures that grew out of a crisis situation and did not reflect a well-thought-out plan. Only with time did the policies evolve into a more permanent system. At this point, however, the role of special interests became more important. Once the system of import restrictions was established, special interests had a stake in seeing the status quo continue, and then they posed an obstacle to any dismantling of the trade barriers. Thus, special interests played less of a role in creating and more of a role in perpetuating the trade barriers that had sprung up in late 1931.

To conclude, the protectionism that emerged at this time stemmed in large part from international monetary problems with the gold standard. Gustav Cassel, who had foreseen many of these problems and warned of a possible depression, also observed the protectionist bias of the gold standard in a deflationary situation:

The gold standard has shown a marked tendency to encourage protectionism. The dread of losing gold is presumably at the bottom of most protectionist measures. Some countries are in fact using such a policy with the direct aim of increasing their gold stocks. And practically all countries on a gold standard consider themselves obliged to defend it by a protectionist system designed to safeguard the balance of trade. International commerce has thus reverted to the primitive view of the early days of the mercantile system, that it is necessary to protect oneself, in relation to every other country, against what is called an adverse balance of trade. Thus we have seen how one country after another is demanding that each foreign country shall buy at least as much from it as it sells to it. This is, of course, ultimately due to a dread of losing gold. Attempts to hinder the export of capital are being made for similar reasons. In this way we have found ourselves driven into a general system of restrictions on commerce and movements of capital, the effects of which are proving, in increasing measure, to be disastrous for the entire world economy. (Cassel 1934, 47)

As noted earlier, the gold standard as a fixed exchange rate regime promoted the growth of world trade prior to World

War I. Yet when it encountered problems in the early 1930s, the gold standard bred protectionism that inflicted great damage on world trade. For this reason, Eichengreen and Temin (2010) refer to the "dual personality" of fixed exchange rates—the fact that they facilitate trade in good times but intensify problems in bad times. While fixed exchange rates do promote trade, the 1930s experience also suggests that countries will use import restrictions as a way of maintaining fixed exchange rates and addressing balance-of-payments difficulties. The logic of this conclusion becomes apparent when we consider the open economy trilemma.

The Open Economy Trilemma

The spread of protectionism is relatively easy to describe, but only through the use of a conceptual framework can we move beyond description and really begin to understand why events played out the way they did. The open economy trilemma provides such a framework.

Policymakers are often confronted with trade-offs in trying to achieve different macroeconomic objectives. In his *Tract on Monetary Reform* (1923), for example, John Maynard Keynes highlighted the conflict between stable exchange rates and stable internal prices. Keynes noted that a country whose central bank was devoted to fixing the value of its currency in terms of gold could not also use monetary policy to ensure stable domestic prices. Alternatively, a country whose central bank had the objective of stabilizing domestic prices could not be assured of having stable exchange rates. Although stable internal prices and stable external prices were considered desirable goals, monetary policy could achieve one or the other, but not both at the same time. Keynes made a strong case for choosing stable internal prices as the objective of policymakers, which is why he opposed going back on the gold standard after World War I.

In an early draft of his classic 1953 essay, "The Case for Flexible Exchange Rates," Milton Friedman referred to the dilemma posed by Keynes. Friedman observed that Keynes had taken open trade policies for granted. But during the 1930s, countries tried to overcome the dilemma and achieve both internal and external price stability through restrictions on trade and payments. By suppressing imports in the hopes of generating a trade surplus and a net inflow of gold, or by restricting other foreign exchange transactions (including capital movements) for the same purpose, a country could, in principle, achieve both objectives—keep the exchange rate fixed and have an independent monetary policy. Therefore, because countries had opened the door to regulating international transactions, Friedman argued that the macroeconomic dilemma "has become a trilemma: fixed exchange rates, stable internal prices, unrestricted multilateral trade; of this trio, any pair is attainable; all three are not simultaneously attainable."[17]

Friedman was not the first to make this point. A few years earlier, Frank Graham (1949, 27) had observed: "Uncoordinated national monetary policies, non-discriminatory, multilateral trade on the basis of free enterprise, and exchange rates fixed, even provisionally, cannot be made to mix. We must choose between them."[18] And before him, James Meade

---

17. I thank Russell Boyer of the University of Western Ontario for providing me with a copy of this early draft from the Milton Friedman papers at the Hoover Institution. Unfortunately, this text was not included in the published version of his essay, although its reasoning is implicit.

18. Graham (1949, 18, 27) continued: "We should know that we must either forgo fixed exchange rates or national monetary sovereignty if we are to avoid the disruption of equilibrium in freely conducted international trade or the systems of controls and inhibitions which is the only alternative when

had considered the trade-offs in using exchange rate changes versus import controls as a means of achieving balance-of-payments adjustment, concluding that "the method of exchange rate adjustment is to be greatly preferred to that of direct trade controls" (Meade 1948, 110).[19] In considering these policy trade-offs, Meade, Graham, and Friedman were among the few economists in the late 1940s and early 1950s to oppose fixed exchange rates and support flexible exchange rates. They advocated flexible exchange rates because it allowed countries to pursue independent monetary policies while also preserving open trade.[20]

The trilemma depicted in figure 1.1 provides a useful way of thinking about the policy choices available to countries during the Great Depression.[21] In particular, it shows how a country's stance with regard to monetary and exchange rate

the internal values of independent currencies deviate—as they always tend to do—from what was, perhaps, a correct relationship when the fixed rates of exchange were set up."

19. Meade's classic work on this topic was his pathbreaking 1952 book, *The Balance of Payments*, which helped him earn the Nobel Prize in 1977 (shared with Bertil Ohlin). In it, Meade distinguished between internal and external balance and argued in favor of exchange rate adjustments to achieve the latter.

20. Another notable economist in this camp, Lloyd Mints (1950, 90), wrote about the "irreconcilable conflict between the requirements for international equilibrium and for domestic stability" that came with fixed exchange rates.

21. The trilemma most often analyzed in recent years is somewhat different. Obstfeld and Taylor (1998) discuss the "impossible trinity" of capital mobility, fixed exchange rates, and independent monetary policy. Obstfeld, Shambaugh, and Taylor (2004) find strong evidence that this trilemma was also a binding constraint on policy during the interwar period. This form of the trilemma is even more appropriate for the post–World War II period because the GATT (now the WTO) helps ensure that world trade will be relatively open. Padoa-Shioppa (1988, 373) proposed an expanded version of the trilemma, the "inconsistent quartet" of free trade, capital mobility, a fixed exchange rate, and an independent monetary policy, in which only three of the four objectives are obtainable.

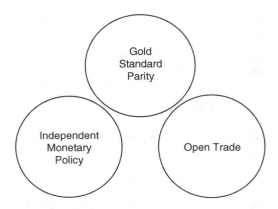

Figure 1.1
The interwar policy trilemma

policy shaped its subsequent trade policy choices. If the gold standard was taken for granted and maintaining the fixed exchange rate of the gold parity was given top priority, a country would have to give up either an independent monetary policy or an open trade policy. In normal times, when the gold standard was functioning well and ensured stable domestic prices, countries had little problem giving up monetary policy independence because there would be no conflict between the fixed exchange rate and stable domestic prices. Therefore, trade could be kept open.

But when the gold standard entered into a deflationary phase, the fixed gold parity did not provide domestic price stability. Because deflation was bound up with the severe economic slump, the economic and political costs of maintaining the gold parity and forgoing domestic price stability began to escalate. Soon, domestic price stability began to supersede exchange rate stability as the most important economic objective, shifting the choices in the trilemma. Then countries could either maintain the gold parity and impose protectionist measures, or allow the currency to depreciate and keep trade open. Some countries were determined to stay on the gold standard, opting to keep the gold parity and sacrifice open trade. Other countries abandoned the gold standard and allowed their currencies to depreciate, enabling them to keep trade relatively open.

The trilemma is rooted in the balance of payments, which can be explained with reference the following equation:

Exports – Imports + Net Capital Inflows = Δ Gold Reserves.

If a country had a balance of trade surplus in which exports exceeded imports, its gold reserves would increase because it would receive more in payments from other countries than it would spend on goods from other countries. By contrast, if exports fell short of imports, then the country's payments would exceed its receipts and its gold reserves would decline, unless capital inflows made up the difference.

This equation for the balance of payments illustrates how trade flows—and hence trade policy, which influences those flows—were linked to monetary policy. Under the gold standard, changes in gold reserves were a key determinant of domestic monetary conditions; a country gaining reserves could have a more expansionary policy, while a country losing reserves would have to tighten policy. If a country's exports fell short of its imports, which was Britain's problem after it overvalued the pound in 1925, the country would lose gold reserves and be forced to tighten monetary policy. If a country's net capital inflows turned negative, which was Germany's problem after the United States cut back its foreign lending in 1928–1929, the country would similarly lose gold reserves and be forced to tighten monetary policy.

To prevent a loss of reserves and its deflationary monetary consequences, a country had several options. It could devalue its currency, that is, raise the statutory price of its currency in terms of gold so as to stimulate exports and discourage imports. It could abandon the gold parity and allow the value of its currency to be determined by the market, eliminating the need for the government to hold gold reserves since it gave up responsibility for maintaining the gold parity. It could default on foreign debts, which would reduce capital outflows. It could restrict spending on foreign goods through import controls, or boost exports through subsidies. Any of these measures could conceivably improve the balance of payments, stem the loss of reserves, and thereby mitigate, if not reverse, deflation.

Other considerations might restrict some of these options. For example, public discussion over the possibility of a devaluation was impossible because it would lead to currency flight and therefore force the government to devalue.[22] A sovereign debt default might be ruled out because it would then cut the country off from international capital markets for some period of time. If the policy options of exchange rate changes or debt default were ruled out, then it is easy to see why countries might turn to trade policies—import controls and export subsidies—to alter trade flows with the hope of boosting its gold reserves.[23] Thus, under fixed exchange rates, trade policy is indirectly linked, but linked nonetheless, to monetary policy.

---

22. Feenstra (1985) shows that countries might be reluctant to devalue and instead resort to trade controls because of the problems caused by currency flight if a devaluation is anticipated.
23. In practice, because export subsidies were costly at a time when countries were trying to reduce budget deficits, countries imposed measures to restrict imports, including tariffs, which raised revenue for the government.

How did these choices play out during the Great Depression? In 1929, most countries were on the gold standard, meaning that they did not have an independent monetary policy. When the worldwide deflation began in mid-1929, they no longer had domestic price stability. In the face of declining gold reserves, as gold was flowing to the United States and France only to be sterilized, a country had to decide whether or not it would defend the exchange rate parity by increasing interest rates and tightening monetary policy. Initially, policymakers did so without hesitation because the gold standard was regarded as a sacred monetary contract. The contract required the central bank to maintain a fixed parity of its currency to gold and to permit the convertibility of its currency into gold. To go off the gold standard, either by changing the parity or by ending convertibility, would have been considered a breach of faith that could be justified only in extreme circumstances, such as war. Leaving the gold standard under any other circumstances, it was believed, would undermine people's confidence and trust in their government and jeopardize monetary and financial stability.

This stubborn attachment to the gold standard, what Eichengreen and Temin (2000) call the "gold standard mentality," had disastrous consequences. But it makes some sense in the historical context of the time when the monetary instability of the early 1920s was recent memory. The German hyperinflation, which destroyed the savings of the middle class and brought economic havoc and political turmoil, continued to haunt policymakers. Austria, Hungary, and Poland also suffered from hyperinflation and its terrible consequences. Although most countries avoided the worst, France, Belgium, and others also had great difficulty controlling inflation and restoring monetary stability. In the public mind, high inflation and the rapid fall in the value of the currency were linked.

Because people often mistakenly thought that a depreciation of the exchange rate caused the high inflation, rather than the reverse, they saw the gold standard as ensuring monetary stability. And countries that did not experience hyperinflation or high inflation during or after World War I observed the trauma of those that did. As a result, they too developed a deep-seated fear of inflation.[24]

This belief in the safety of the gold standard explains why governments were reluctant to abandon the gold parity. Straumann (2009, 616) makes the striking observation that "not a single European country deliberately devalued its currency in the 1930s." Policymakers feared that untethering one's currency from gold would be a leap in the dark, leading to monetary chaos and bringing political and social upheaval. They resisted a fall in the value of their currency because they feared its inflationary consequences. Such inflation, they thought, would reduce real wages, destroy savings, ruin the middle class, and otherwise make matters worse. "An overwhelming majority of central bankers, national politicians, business executives, and union leaders, regardless of the economic structure of their countries, defended gold parity because of their sincere belief that a devaluation would not improve but would deteriorate the situation," Straumann (2009, 132) notes. Therefore, "a government took such a dramatic step only when forced to do so by a dramatic loss of reserves, a severe banking crisis or a devaluation of the currency of a major trading partner." For this reason, most

---

24. As was pointed out in a League of Nations (1938, 10) report, "there emerged in the countries whose currencies had collapsed only a few years before a firm determination not to let it happen again. The destruction of savings and the economic disorganization produced by the inflations had wrought such havoc that this quite naturally appeared to be the basic evil which must be avoided at all costs. There was, indeed, in many of these countries, a tendency to identify inflation with devaluation."

countries were driven off the gold standard only when their gold reserves came perilously close to exhaustion.

Despite the gold standard's importance and the efforts made to keep it intact, the pressures of financial crises and deflation became so strong that eventually every country was driven off it. The first group of countries that went off the gold standard, the exchange control group, experienced financial crises, runs on their currencies, and a massive loss of reserves. Most of these countries did not go off the gold standard by ending the fixed parity of their currency in terms of gold. Instead, they imposed exchange controls that severed the convertibility of their currencies into gold while keeping the official exchange rate parity intact. These exchange controls were used to stop capital flight and the drain on the country's reserves. Germany was the first to do so, in July 1931, followed by other Central European countries that experienced a drain of gold reserves after Britain left the gold standard in September, including Austria, Bulgaria, Czechoslovakia, Denmark, Estonia, Greece, Hungary, Italy, Latvia, Lithuania, Poland, Romania, Turkey, and Yugoslavia. Many of the countries that adopted exchange controls had experienced hyperinflation in the early 1920s. Therefore, they were extremely worried about any depreciation of their currency, and they preserved the formal gold parity as a symbol of monetary stability.[25]

The second set of countries, the sterling bloc, abandoned the gold standard by giving up on the gold parity and

---

25. "It was only natural that European countries which had undergone runaway inflations during the early 1920s should regard exchange control as the lesser of the two evils," Henderson (1955, 246) noted. "In Central European eyes, accordingly, inflation and exchange depreciation had become virtually synonymous terms of terrible significance."

allowing their currencies to depreciate on foreign exchange markets. The sterling bloc was led by Britain, which gave up the parity in September 1931, and included such countries as Sweden, Denmark, Norway, Finland, Japan, Portugal, Egypt, Greece, Bolivia, Peru, Thailand, and Latvia. Britain never seriously considered imposing exchange controls because it could not regulate capital movements and still maintain its position as the world's leading international financial center. When it was clear that the run on the pound would deplete its gold reserves, the Bank of England simply stopped supporting the pound and allowed it to depreciate on foreign exchange markets. That changed the rate at which the currency could be exchanged for gold, without interfering with the convertibility of its currency in terms of gold.

Another set of countries, the gold bloc, had enough reserves in 1931 that they did not have to consider leaving the gold standard either by changing the parity or by ending convertibility. The gold bloc was led by France and included Belgium, Italy, the Netherlands, Poland, and Switzerland. However, once the sterling bloc countries allowed their currencies to depreciate, the gold bloc currencies became overvalued. They began to experience balance-of-payments problems, gold outflows, and deflation, and hence they turned to import restrictions to mitigate these problems. Such restrictions failed to relieve the deflationary pressure and end the slump. As a result, the gold bloc disintegrated over time. Italy imposed capital controls in May 1934, as did Poland in April 1936. Belgium allowed its currency to depreciate in March 1935, as did France and the remaining gold bloc countries in September 1936.

Not all countries fit neatly into these three categories. Some commodity-exporting countries, such as Argentina and Australia, had suffered a severe deterioration in their terms of trade as a result of the collapse in agricultural and raw materials prices and went off the gold standard as early as December 1929. The United States stood apart from these groups but went off the gold standard in April 1933 and allowed its currency to depreciate. Canada guided its exchange rate to a middle ground between sterling and the dollar. And some countries shifted from one group to another, or straddled them. Italy was initially a member of the gold bloc but later imposed exchange controls rather than allow its currency to depreciate. Denmark followed the sterling bloc in terms of exchange rate policy, but also resorted to strict exchange controls.

Still, by the end of 1931, most countries had segregated themselves into one of the three groups: the exchange control group (which ended gold convertibility), the sterling bloc (which ended the gold parity), and the gold bloc (which stayed on the gold standard). Figure 1.2 shows the decision tree of policy choices that produced these outcomes. When countries were faced with intensified deflationary pressure in 1931, they first had to decide if they would maintain the gold parity. Britain and the sterling bloc chose not to, and let the exchange rate go. The depreciation of their currencies relieved deflationary pressure and resolved their balance-of-payments difficulties without the need for trade restrictions. Countries that decided to maintain the gold parity had two choices: they could continue to allow capital mobility and use trade controls to regulate the balance of payments, or they could block the movement of capital and use exchange controls to regulate the balance of payments. France and the gold bloc opted for the former, while Germany and the exchange control group opted for the latter. Because trade controls and exchange controls reduce spending on imports, they both constituted "protectionist" policies.

Figure 1.2
Economic policy choices

Thus, in practical terms, unless countries were willing to submit to continued deflation and balance-of-payments problems, the trilemma was really a dilemma: countries had to change the exchange rate (depreciation) or change their trade policy (protectionism).

What determined the segregation of countries into these three groups? The selection process was not random. Instead, the main factor was a country's recent experience with inflation. As Barry Eichengreen (1992, 394) has noted:

The single best predictor of which countries in the 1930s allowed their currencies to depreciate and pursued reflationary initiatives, instead of clinging to the gold standard or adopting equally stifling exchange controls, was the experience with inflation a decade before. Countries that had endured persistent inflation in the 1920s were loath to permit currency depreciation and to expand their money supplies. They continued to associate depreciation and monetary expansion with inflation, even in the midst of the most catastrophic deflation of the twentieth century. They showed remarkable persistence in rejecting arguments for devaluation and reflation in the face of incontrovertible evidence of their beneficial effects in other countries.

For example, although the Bank of England was concerned about inflation, Britain did not have a serious problem with inflation after World War I, and it was less concerned about a depreciation of its currency than most other European countries. On the other hand, Germany's experience with hyperinflation made it extremely cautious about jeopardizing its hard won monetary stability.

By the end of the 1930s, every major country had allowed its currency to depreciate relative to its gold parity, with the exception of those in the exchange control group. Figure 1.3 shows the exchange rates of the leading countries relative to the 1929 gold parity. Britain allowed the pound to depreciate in September 1931. The United States suspended gold convertibility and allowed the dollar to depreciate in April 1933. France allowed the franc to fall in value in September 1936. Germany ended convertibility in July 1931, but never altered the official exchange rate peg. The main factor determining when a country departed from the gold standard was the extent of deflationary pressure that it faced; other factors were the presence of a banking crisis, the ability of the central bank to defend the gold parity (the amount of reserves covering central bank liabilities), the political regime (democracies left the gold standard earlier than authoritarian governments), and the independence of the central bank.[26]

---

26. See Wolf and Yousef (2007), Wandschneider (2008), and Wolf (2008).

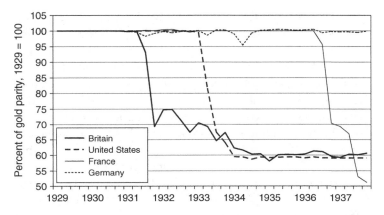

Figure 1.3
Exchange rates, 1929–1937. *Source:* League of Nations (1940).

But the main focus here is how a country's choice regarding the gold standard and its exchange rate influenced its trade policy. The implication of the trilemma is that countries that allowed their currency to depreciate (the sterling bloc) should have avoided using many protectionist measures, while those that maintained the gold parity and kept their exchange rate fixed (the exchange control group and the gold bloc) would have imposed many restrictions on international trade. The next two chapters explore this implication in greater detail.

Conclusion

This chapter has provided a narrative account of how protectionism arose in the early 1930s, particularly after the disintegration of the gold standard in 1931. The explanation for the outbreak of protectionism is framed not in terms of special interest politics but in terms of macroeconomic policy choices. The open economy trilemma implies that countries could achieve only two of three objectives: a stable exchange rate, stable internal prices, and open trade. When the gold standard worked well, there was no major trade-off among these objectives: stable exchange rates delivered stable domestic prices, and so trade could be kept open. With the onset of deflation in the late 1920s and early 1930s, the stable exchange rates of the gold standard no longer guaranteed stable domestic prices. As domestic price stability became a priority, countries had the choice of keeping the gold parity or open trade policies. Why different countries resolved the trilemma differently, and the implications for trade policy, is the story for the next chapter.

2   Resolving the Trilemma: Protection or Depreciation?

The previous chapter described how the protectionism of the 1930s was rooted in the macroeconomic policy choices that countries faced when confronted with a large deflationary shock under the gold standard. Countries had to decide whether to maintain the fixed exchange rate of their currency in terms of the gold parity or to abandon the gold standard and allow their currency to fall in value. This choice had enormous implications for trade policy. Countries that allowed their currencies to depreciate resolved their balance-of-payments problems and, according to the trilemma, should have been able to keep trade relatively open. Countries maintaining their gold parity suffered from overvalued currencies, which exacerbated their balance-of-payments problems and led them to impose severe import restrictions.

This chapter examines how these policy choices were resolved differently by different countries, focusing on Britain and the sterling bloc, Germany and the exchange control group, the United States, and finally France and the gold bloc. Each group had similar trade-offs regarding exchange rate policy and trade policy, but each resolved the trilemma differently based on its recent history, its immediate circumstances, and its political institutions.

Britain and the Sterling Bloc

From the mid-nineteenth century up to the Great Depression, British policymakers were guided by the "Victorian consensus" about what constituted good and virtuous economic policy.[1] The four cornerstones of the Victorian consensus were the gold standard, free trade, balanced budgets, and limited government.

Although it left the gold standard during World War I, Britain was certain to rejoin it after the war. The only question was whether it would do so at the prewar parity or at a depreciated rate. John Maynard Keynes and others argued that value of the pound in terms of gold should be lower than before the war because British prices were higher than their prewar level. This meant that restoring the prewar parity would leave the pound overvalued; British prices would be higher in comparison to other countries' prices, leading to trade deficits, a loss of gold reserves, and deflationary pressure. Despite these potential problems, Chancellor of the Exchequer Winston Churchill agreed with other government experts who argued that the prewar parity should be restored. In 1925, Britain rejoined the gold standard at the prewar parity.

This decision meant that British export industries had difficulty competing on the world market, and some domestic industries faced greater competition from imports. This made it more difficult for Britain to maintain balance-of-payments equilibrium, and therefore put pressure on the country's gold reserves. The Bank of England was forced to raise interest rates to support the pound, but this discouraged

---

1. The term "Victorian consensus" invites comparison to the "Washington consensus" of the 1990s, the set of "good" economic policies endorsed by Washington-based institutions such as the U.S. Treasury, the World Bank, and the International Monetary Fund.

domestic investment and weakened the economy. The deflationary pressure also aggravated unemployment because workers resisted any reduction in nominal wages as a way of bringing down costs. In fact, Keynes (1925) had warned that Britain's decision to rejoin the gold standard at an overvalued rate would amount to "the deliberate intensification of unemployment."

The exchange rate decision, and the difficulties in deflating British wages and prices to restore equilibrium, helped put the economy in a deep slump. The social distress that followed Britain's decision is illustrated by the violent and divisive 1926 General Strike. These economic troubles put the Victorian consensus under extreme pressure. The existing policy framework seemed to offer no solution to the country's economic problems. After many years, deflation and nonintervention had failed to restore an equilibrium that approached full employment.[2] As political pressure on the government to do something about the slump mounted, the question became which cornerstone of the Victorian consensus would give way first.

In 1929, the British government set up the Committee on Finance and Industry, known as the Macmillan Committee, to give advice on how to escape from the country's economic predicament. The committee included representatives from the business and financial community, as well as government officials and economists. Foremost among them was John Maynard Keynes. Acutely aware of the policy dilemmas, Keynes would prove very influential in framing and evaluating the policy choices that Britain faced.

In February 1930, Keynes laid out the policy options in evidence given before the committee. He recommended against

---

2. Generous unemployment benefits also contributed to the high rate of unemployment; see Feinstein, Temin, and Toniolo (2008).

devaluation on the grounds that the British government was firmly committed to remaining on the gold standard. He refused to reopen the question of the proper exchange rate, saying that the government's decision had been made and was irreversible. This was an unusual position for Keynes to take because he had opposed returning to the gold standard after World War I, particularly at the prewar parity in 1925. But now, in addition to accepting the government's position, he argued that the costs of departing from the gold standard would outweigh the benefits because the burden of servicing Britain's short-term foreign currency debts would increase by the amount by which the pound fell in value. This would put an additional burden on the public finances and complicate the country's balance-of-payments situation. Furthermore, it would be a breach of faith with Britain's creditors, a violation of trust that would damage London's reputation as a financial center.

Keynes also ruled out a coordinated central bank policy of revaluing gold that would allow for monetary reflation. France and the United States would refuse to cooperate, he expected, making this impossible. Keynes noted that the trade deficit and associated outflow of gold could be reduced by cutting production costs and thereby increasing exports. However, each of the ways in which this cost-cutting could be accomplished—by reducing money wages, improving productivity, or subsidizing business output—was problematic.

Keynes then offered his "own favorite remedy," subsidies to domestic investment, though he conceded there was not much political support for the idea. According to the prevailing fiscal orthodoxy, the government should reduce its spending to rein in the growing budget deficit. Consequently, there was little enthusiasm for a big expansion in government spending and borrowing to finance the public investments that Keynes wanted. According to "the Treasury view," government spending would simply crowd out private spending and fail to give the economy a boost.

Finally, Keynes raised the controversial issue of a revenue tariff. He thought that such a tariff would reduce imports and improve the balance of trade, and thus shrink or reverse gold outflows. Reducing imports might also stimulate domestic production to the extent that domestic goods were a good substitute for foreign goods. Of course, he was aware that a tariff would harm economic efficiency in the long run and give rise to vested interests that would want to make the policy permanent. "I am frightfully afraid of protection as a long-term policy, but we cannot afford always to take the long views," he observed. "The question, in my opinion, is how far I am prepared to risk long-period disadvantages in order to get some help to the immediate position" (Keynes 1971–1988, 20:120).

In sum, there seemed to be no good options. Most members of the Committee on Finance and Industry, especially those from the financial sector and the government, agreed with Keynes that leaving the gold standard was unthinkable. However, Ernest Bevin, the leader of the Trade Union Congress and later foreign minister, openly questioned the wisdom of staying on the gold standard. He maintained that returning to the gold standard had worked out well for the City of London but was a disaster for the rest of the country. Bevin was particularly concerned that Britain had suffered from an industrial depression since 1925. He argued that the committee should "go to the root of the problem" and rid the country of the "monetary straightjacket" by ditching the gold standard (Boyce 1987, 282, 293). Bevin wondered why that option was not on the table: "In all our discussions we seem quite willing to face an industrial upheaval or a decrease of wages; but we are simply terror-stricken at touching the rentier, or the value of the pound."

With various domestic policies ruled out as politically infeasible, the options seemed to narrow to just two: leaving the gold standard or abandoning free trade. Some committee members began to recognize this policy dilemma. As this exchange reveals, some of them indicated their preference for keeping trade free over maintaining the gold standard:

Bradbury   I am afraid of tampering with Free Trade, and I am also afraid of tampering with the gold standard. If I had to choose between tampering with the gold standard as a remedy and Protection, I should be solid for tampering with the gold standard. I should much prefer it to Protection.

Bevin   I agree.

Lubbock   I should be very sorry to think that that the choice of one of those was the dilemma.

Bradbury   So should I.

Bevin   I think it is bound to be one of [those] two things.[3]

Despite his previous skepticism about the gold standard, Keynes resisted this line of thought. He reiterated that the decision to go back to gold had been made and that it would be irresponsible to reverse it. Any breach of the gold parity would lead to consequences "too appalling to contemplate." He also warned against publicly discussing the question because if investors knew that such a step was being contemplated, it would immediately trigger a mass selling of pounds for gold, which would exhaust Britain's gold reserves and force a devaluation. Indeed, it was difficult for government officials to debate the pros and cons of a devaluation because

---

3. Quoted in Clarke (1988, 210).

if word leaked that such a step was being considered, it could trigger a speculative attack against the pound sterling.

In the end, however, the committee did not believe that going off the gold standard was a realistic option. In its final report, the committee mentioned the possibility of a devaluation, but concluded, "We have no hesitation in rejecting this course" (Committee on Finance and Industry 1931, 110). The foundation of international trade, finance, and commerce, the report maintained, is confidence, something that depended on the value of the currency being certain over time.[4]

Meanwhile, faced with the choice of abandoning the gold standard or abandoning free trade, Keynes soon came to the view that free trade should be ditched. Keynes first made his case to government officials behind closed doors. By July 1930, Keynes had "become reluctantly convinced that some protectionist measures should be introduced," but he made it clear that this conclusion arose from "a question of *choice* between alternatives, none of which are attractive in themselves." He proposed a 10 percent import tariff and a 10 percent subsidy to exports, which he said would be equivalent to a 10 percent devaluation.[5]

In March 1931, writing in *The New Statesman and the Nation*, Keynes went public with his support for a revenue tariff. He argued that business profitability had to be restored so that firms could expand and start hiring workers and thereby reduce unemployment. For this to occur, either

---

4. Bevin and another committee member added a reservation, noting that monetary policy was examined only in the context of the gold standard. They pointed out that if international cooperation was impossible, then "a point may be reached when this country may be compelled to go off the present form of the gold standard," but they did not explicitly advocate that view (Committee on Finance and Industry 1931, 240).
5. See Eichengreen (1984) and Irwin (1996) for discussions of Keynes's views on trade policy.

prices had to rise (the expansionist cure) or costs had to fall
(the contractionist cure). Keynes rejected the contractionist
cure: reducing costs through wage reductions would lead
to "social injustice and violent resistance" and should be
avoided. Keynes embraced the expansionist cure, but noted
that it would create problems for the trade balance and the
government's fiscal position. He pointed out that "a policy
of expansion sufficiently drastic to be useful" might drive
the country off the gold standard because it would diminish
investor confidence in the pound. Because Keynes believed
that leaving the gold standard was undesirable, he insisted
that "our exchange position should be relentlessly defended"
so that Britain could maintain its financial leadership in the
world (Keynes 1931a).

To neutralize the pressure that an expansionist policy
would have on the balance of payments, Keynes advocated "a
substantial revenue tariff." He proposed a flat tax on imports
of 15 percent on manufactured goods and 5 percent on food-
stuffs and certain raw materials. Once prices had returned
to their 1929 level, the tariff could be removed. He argued
that a revenue tariff would promote economic recovery by
increasing prices and by shifting demand from foreign goods
to domestic goods. A tariff had the additional advantage of
raising revenue and strengthening the country's fiscal position; hence, "compared with any alternative which is open to
us, this measure is unique in that it would at the same time
relieve the pressing problems of the budget and restore business confidence."

Keynes's public advocacy of protectionism was heresy to
proponents of economic orthodoxy and the Victorian consensus. Free trade had been an article of faith in British politics
since the repeal of the Corn Laws in 1846. Keynes's apostasy
generated consternation among other economists, most of

whom endorsed both the gold standard and free trade.[6] The director of the London School of Economics, William Beveridge, organized a group of leading economists, including Lionel Robbins and John Hicks, to collaborate on a book, *Tariffs: The Case Examined*, that rebutted Keynes and called his remedy "inappropriate and harmful." Mainstream economic opinion refused to consider any changes to the gold standard or free trade, but it failed to come to terms with the circumstances in which Britain found itself and ignored the trade-offs among different policies.

Keynes's public call for a revenue tariff also gave intellectual ammunition to protectionist business interests and the Conservative Party. For decades, the Liberal and Labour parties had strongly supported free trade, while the Conservatives flirted with protection and imperial preferences. The Conservatives had lost several general elections when they had campaigned on a platform of fair trade and imperial preferences. But the intensification of foreign competition after World War I, and particularly the overvaluation of the pound in 1925, generated increasing support among some business leaders for a modification of Britain's free trade policy.

As the debate about Britain's policy options continued, the government failed to act decisively, and its inaction was soon overtaken by events. After the crises in Austria and Germany in the summer of 1931, the Bank of England's gold reserve position began to deteriorate. A government report in July said that, unless expenditure reductions were undertaken, the fiscal deficit would be unexpectedly large. This news contributed to a run on the pound, which caused Britain's gold

---

6. In addition to his firm endorsement of free trade, Lionel Robbins (1934, 117) argued that "no really impartial observer of world events can do other than regard the abandonment of the gold standard by Great Britain as a catastrophe of the first order of magnitude."

This David Low cartoon ("And so to bed") was published in the *Evening Standard* on September 14, 1931. It shows John Maynard Keynes in the tariff bed as sleepwalking politicians move to join him and others at peace with the policy. *Source:* British Cartoon Archive, University of Kent. Reproduced with permission from Associated Newspapers Ltd.,/Solo Syndication.

reserves to fall sharply. In August 1931, the government proposed fiscal austerity and retrenchment measures. But the flight from the pound only intensified, indicative of the financial market's intolerance of the government's fiscal position.[7]

7. According to Sayers (1976, 2:390), the explanation for the behavior of financial markets lay "in memories of the currency disorders of the early twenties, which were, after all, less than ten years behind. In those troublesome times it had become accepted doctrine that an uncorrected budget deficit is the root of forced increase in the supply of money and depreciation of the currency, and that such depreciations become almost if not quite unmanageable. This view was not a mere academic fetish: it permeated the atmosphere in all financial markets."

Writing in the *Evening Standard* in early September 1931, Keynes said that he now believed a devaluation was the right remedy. However, if the government was determined to remain on the gold standard, the country would have to take immediate steps to improve the balance of trade and stem the gold outflow. In his view, there were two policy options: reduce all money wages in the country or restrict imports. Given the "appallingly difficult" problems with the former, Keynes argued "it would be crazy not to try first the effects of the alternative, and much milder, measure of restricting imports" (Keynes 1931b).

Britain's foreign exchange crisis came to a head in mid-September as the loss of reserves accelerated. The Bank of England failed to secure loans from other central banks to sustain the gold parity. The idea of imposing exchange controls was rejected without much consideration.[8] After years of fighting to support the pound, using high interest rates in an effort to deflate wages and prices and restore equilibrium, government officials had lost their resolve. They were no longer willing to continue supporting the currency in view of the high unemployment that the British economy had suffered with for so long (Eichengreen and Jeanne 2000).

Therefore, over a weekend, Bank of England and Treasury officials made the decision to suspend the convertibility of

---

8. Sayers (1976, 2:411) notes that the question of exchange controls was raised in August 1931, but officials "who appreciated the ramifications of the international use of sterling naturally suspected that no simple system of control would be appropriate, and without much discussion the idea was left on one side." As Hubert Henderson (1955, 247), an economist in the British government around this time, added, "The traditions of London as a financial centre, in which foreigners were accustomed to deposit large balances on the understanding that they could withdraw them readily on the shortest notice, were enough in Great Britain in September 1931 to make the idea of exchange control unthinkable." According to Leith-Ross (1968, 140), Keynes urged the imposition of exchange controls to save the pound during the weekend the gold standard was abandoned, but this advice was summarily rejected.

pounds into gold at the fixed parity. On Monday, September 21, Britain left the gold standard, and the pound was allowed to depreciate on foreign exchange markets. To everyone's astonishment, a major pillar of the Victorian consensus had crumbled. "No one told us we could do that" was the reaction of one former government official (Eichengreen and Temin 2000). Yet, as the pound fell in value against other currencies, the fears of those who insisted that Britain must remain on the gold standard did not come true, and the economy even began to revive.

The trilemma suggests, and Keynes certainly recognized, that currency depreciation and import restrictions were substitutes for one another. As he wrote immediately after the decision to leave the gold standard, "proposals for high protection have ceased to be urgent" (Keynes 1971–1988, 9:243). Keynes argued that "the depreciation of sterling readjusts British costs to world costs far more effectively than a tariff could, and has greatly weakened the case for protective duties" (ibid., 21:103). But in terms of actual policy, the dilemma was not resolved in a clear-cut way. Not only did Britain abandon the gold standard, it soon imposed a higher tariff as well. Instead of giving up either the gold standard or free trade, it gave up both. What explains this unusual combination of policies?[9]

Part of the explanation is that the departure from the gold standard caught everyone by surprise. Because the gold standard had been expected to remain intact, Keynes's advocacy and other political forces had built momentum for the imposition of a tariff. A key political change allowed this to happen. In August 1931, just as the foreign exchange pressures on the pound were intensifying, the Labour government collapsed.

---

9. For different takes on this question, see Eichengreen (1981), Williamson (1992), and Garside (1998).

Having opposed both a revenue tariff and cuts in unemployment benefits, the government proved unable to address the nation's deteriorating finances. A coalition "national government," including Liberals and Conservatives, allowed Labour Prime Minister Ramsay Macdonald to stay in office, provided there was an early election. In late October, a general election returned the National government to office, but gave the Conservatives much more power within the coalition.

The election of a Conservative-dominated government increased the likelihood of some sort of tariff being imposed, despite Britain's departure from the gold standard just weeks earlier. In anticipation of such an event, British imports increased markedly. Parliament responded by immediately enacting the Abnormal Importations Act, which permitted the Board of Trade to impose duties up to 100 percent on imports found to have been "dumped" on the British market.

Yet the surge in imports outstripped the growth of exports, which the depreciation of the pound would promote, but only with a lag. The deterioration in the trade balance raised questions about whether the pound would have to fall even more, or whether it would succeed in restoring balanced trade. In response to these developments, in February 1932 Parliament enacted the Import Duties Act, which imposed a general, across-the-board tariff of 10 percent on imports, with an exemption for raw materials and products from the British Empire.[10] Thus, two major pillars of the Victorian consensus, the gold standard and free trade, crumbled at nearly the same time.

This sequence of events helps us understand the rationale for imposing a tariff after the pound had depreciated in value.

---

10. The legislation also gave authorities the discretion to impose higher duties under certain circumstances. For example, in early 1932, duties on finished iron and steel products were lifted to 20 percent and those on raw iron and steel products to 33⅓ percent.

A key reason why the tariff followed quickly on the heels of Britain's departure from the gold standard is that the government had no confidence that the pound's depreciation would be orderly or would balance trade. In the months after Britain left the gold standard, the balance of trade had deteriorated, prompting fears that the pound might fall even more and raising the risk of increasing import prices and perhaps a surge in inflation. A higher duty on imports was seen as a way of closing the trade gap and supporting the pound. To this explanation can be added that Britain was facing a large fiscal deficit and the government had long desired measures that would enhance revenue, but was wary of increasing domestic taxes or cutting spending on unemployment benefits. Thus, the General Tariff was a fiscal measure that was seen as way to achieve multiple objectives—to increase government revenue (an increase in domestic taxes having been ruled out), close the budget deficit, improve the trade balance, restore confidence in the pound, and give some room for monetary reflation.

To be sure, the General Tariff of 1932 also reflected the growth in protectionist sentiment. And it reflected a desire to create tariff preferences for the British dominions. But the protection of British manufactures from foreign competition was not foremost in the minds of the government officials who crafted the measure. In his study of the British decision to adopt the tariff, Eichengreen (1981, 2) concluded that "the General Tariff was not imposed as an anti-unemployment policy but rather as an attempt to strengthen the trade balance and prevent the exchange rate from depreciating excessively." This was certainly the rationale that Chancellor of the Exchequer Neville Chamberlain gave in introducing the tariff bill in Parliament. Hubert Henderson (1955, 249), who served as secretary of the Economic Advisory Council during this period, recalled that "the British authorities were worried about their capacity to check an undue fall of sterling for several months after our departure from the gold standard. To improve the balance of payments seemed in those circumstances an urgent objective of policy; and this consideration was an important factor, though not the only one, in the introduction of a general tariff in 1932."

Had the Labour government been in power throughout this period, the depreciation of the pound may have sufficed to put tariff proposals to rest. As it happened, the shift in political power to the Conservatives and the adverse turn in the trade balance meant that going off the gold standard did not derail the political momentum that had developed for the imposition of a revenue tariff. As an influential policy adviser, Keynes bears some responsibility for this outcome. As Moggridge (1992, 514) notes, "By refusing openly to advocate devaluation and by lending his public support for protection . . . Keynes helped create a climate of opinion in which, after Britain left gold and did not need protection on Keynes's grounds, she got a highly protective tariff system anyway."

After Britain left the gold standard in the fall of 1931, nearly twenty other countries followed. Some countries, such as Egypt, pegged their currencies to the pound and simply followed its depreciation against other currencies. Other countries, such as Sweden, did not want to leave the gold standard, but foreign exchange market pressure quickly forced them to give up their defense of the gold parity. Sweden's central bank, the Riksbank, survived the chaotic summer of 1931 with little loss of gold and foreign exchange reserves, and market participants expected that Sweden would stay on the gold standard. But Britain's abandonment of its gold parity triggered a massive selloff of the kronor. Despite several interest rate hikes and attempts to obtain international financing, the nation's gold reserves began falling at an accelerating rate. With no letup in sight, Sweden ended gold convertibility just days after Britain did.

Although it did not suffer the same loss of reserves, Norway left the gold standard at about the same time. Finland followed soon after. Yet "the early exit from gold was not the result of a sound strategy developed by Scandinavian central bankers and government officials," Straumann (2010, 94) notes. "On the contrary, they were forced to devalue and felt shocked by the breakdown of the international monetary regime they had helped to rebuild only a few years earlier." In Japan, the situation was similar. After experiencing large gold outflows in October and November 1931, despite interest rate rises, as well as a collapse in the government, Japan suspended gold exports and left the gold standard in December (Metzler 2006).[11]

Unlike Britain, most countries that followed it off the gold standard viewed exchange rate adjustments and trade policy measures as substitutes and alternatives for one another, and therefore opted to keep trade policies relatively open. In Sweden, for example, the exchange rate adjustment made significant import restrictions unnecessary, and it did not significantly increase its tariffs or other trade barriers. However, like Britain, not all countries with depreciated currencies could avoid imposing higher duties. In 1932, Norway increased its duties by about 20 percent for fiscal reasons, much as Britain had, and Finland's tariffs edged up as well.

---

11. Although the Japanese yen depreciated 60 percent in the year after the country left the gold standard in December 1931, the large drop was not engineered by the government as a "competitive devaluation" but reflected the initial overvaluation of the yen and adverse news about Japan's international role (Ito, Okina, and Teranishi 1993).

Even more unusually, Denmark not only allowed its currency to depreciate but also imposed exchange controls that severely reduced spending on imports. As an exporter of agricultural goods, Denmark suffered an especially sharp terms-of-trade shock when the Great Depression hit. Because many of the tariffs and quotas in the early 1930s were aimed at agricultural imports, Denmark's exports were particularly affected, and this impeded the country's ability to earn enough foreign exchange to finance imports. Unlike other sterling bloc countries, Denmark imposed exchange and capital controls and began rationing foreign exchange. By the end of 1931, 95 percent of the value of Danish imports required foreign exchange permits.[12]

The decision to leave the gold standard and allow their currencies to depreciate had implications not only for trade policy but for monetary policy as well. Freed from the mandate to keep the exchange rate fixed, the central banks could ease monetary conditions and focus on domestic price stability. When Britain left the gold standard, the Bank of England initially raised interest rates out of fear that an excessive depreciation of the pound would have inflationary consequences. By February–March 1932, when the dreaded inflation failed to materialize, the bank was able to cut rates sharply. As a result of a more expansionary monetary policy, the deflation ended and prices stabilized. The fall in interest rate began to spur domestic investment, and soon the economy began to recover (Middleton 2010).

---

12. As Salmon (2003, 234) notes, "For Denmark, the depression inaugurated acute problems of adjustment and brought far-reaching institutional changes. . . . Its response was to introduce a system of exchange and import controls which transformed Denmark almost overnight from one of the most liberal economies in Europe to one in which there was 'a greater regulation of economic life than in any other western country with the possible exception of Germany.' The key instrument was the import licensing system introduced in the autumn of 1931."

In announcing the decision to leave gold, Sweden's finance minister stated that the new goal of monetary policy would be to maintain the internal purchasing power of money—in other words, to stabilize the domestic price level (Berg and Jonung 1999). As an informal adviser to the minister, Gustav Cassel was instrumental in making price stability the Riksbank's objective. The announcement of this goal and subsequent monetary policy helped bring deflation to a halt, but also kept inflationary expectations in check. The krona was allowed to float against other currencies from October 1931 to July 1933. After that, and for the remainder of the decade, the krona was pegged to the British pound, a policy that proved to be consistent with price stability. With the more relaxed stance of monetary policy, Sweden's economy, as well as those of others whose currency had depreciated, began to recover.

In sum, Britain and the other countries that left the gold standard and allowed their currencies to depreciate were not always able to avoid imposing protectionist measures. However, as we shall see, in comparison to countries whose currency was not allowed to depreciate, they were able to avoid imposing very severe restrictions on imports.

Germany and the Exchange Control Group

The trilemma was even more of a constraint in Germany and other Central European countries. By refusing to allow their currencies to depreciate, they found it necessary to impose exchange controls, which brutally suppressed their international trade.

As we saw in chapter 1, the problems began in 1928–1929, when U.S. foreign lending declined sharply. Along with the global economic slowdown caused in part by the drain of gold to the United States and France, this helped push

Germany into a recession. As tax revenues fell and expenditures on unemployment relief soared, Germany struggled with a budget imbalance that threatened large increases in government debt.

As politicians grappled with how to address the situation, German politics was thrown into turmoil. Deadlock over Germany's budget situation in early 1930 led to the appointment of Heinrich Brüning as chancellor. Brüning advocated an austerity policy of higher taxes and deep cuts in public spending. In the election of September 1930, the electorate repudiated the government and voters turned in increasing numbers to the Nazis and Communists. The growing prospects of political extremism led to massive selling of the mark, forcing Germany's central bank, the Reichsbank, to raise interest rates. This weakened the economy even further and made the fiscal situation even worse.

Still, Brüning retained enough political support to be reappointed chancellor. Fearful that the unsettling events in Germany might lead to political instability and radicalism, foreign governments backed new loans to Germany. The prospect of Western financial support stabilized the situation for a time. However, the loans were jeopardized when the plans for an Austrian-German customs union leaked out. France's staunch opposition to the union led it to withhold its assistance and the aid package was put in doubt. With the country's fiscal situation continuing to deteriorate, Brüning announced a moratorium on reparations payments. This precipitated a full-blown currency crisis. Germany's gold reserves plunged 40 percent in June 1931 as investors dumped their holdings of marks in exchange for gold. The Reichsbank quickly hiked interest rates, but it did little to stop the mark's slide.

The flight from the mark threatened to exhaust all of Germany's gold and foreign exchange reserves. Emergency credits from the Bank for International Settlements and major central banks were exhausted within days and failed to stop the drain. Germany had few options. It could do nothing and watch its gold and foreign exchange reserves vanish. It could devalue the mark by changing the gold parity. Or it could sever the convertibility of the mark into gold by imposing restrictions on foreign exchange transactions.

Doing nothing was not an option. If it lost all of its reserves, Germany would have no means of paying reparations. Forced to default on its debts, it would be cut off from international capital markets.

Devaluing the mark was not an attractive option either. Reparation payments were fixed in gold terms. Devaluing the mark would have made it much more difficult for Germany to service its obligations. In addition, a devaluation would have stirred memories of the catastrophic hyperinflation of 1923 and the plummeting value of the mark. Untethering the mark from its gold parity would have triggered expectations of renewed monetary instability, including a cycle of further devaluations and accelerating inflation. As James (1986, 390) writes,

There were widespread fears that a devaluation would lead to an uncontrollable slide of the Mark. These may have been the consequence of the recent and painful memories of the inflation and hyperinflation. . . . It was quite realistic to believe that German abandonment of the gold standard would destroy the only precariously restored financial stability of Germany.

For these reasons, a devaluation of the mark was never seriously considered.

The only option seemed to be exchange controls, which would put an immediate end to the loss of gold reserves. Exchange controls were a way of regulating all payments to foreigners, whether for imports or for debt repayment, and meant that the government would take control of all foreign exchange transactions. Exporters would be required to turn over all of their gold and foreign exchange earnings to the government, which would then decide how much to allocate to reparations and debt repayment, the purchase of imports, and so forth. Exchange controls functioned as trade controls because government permission had to be obtained to acquire the foreign exchange necessary to buy foreign goods.

Therefore, in late July 1931, the German government issued a series of emergency decrees that gave the Reichsbank a monopoly over all foreign exchange transactions, prohibited any deviation from the official exchange rate, and abolished the forward market for the mark. While the official rate at which the mark was valued in terms of gold was unchanged, the convertibility of marks into gold was now at the government's discretion. These exchange controls were introduced as an emergency measure. Most observers believed that the controls were temporary and would be abolished once the crisis had passed, at which time convertibility would be restored. Instead, it evolved into a permanent regime for restricting Germany's trade with and payments to the rest of the world.

Two months after Germany imposed exchange controls, Britain and other countries went off the gold standard, and the value of the pound fell against the mark. This made it easier for Germany to repay its sterling-denominated debt. At the same time, the fall in the pound made German goods more expensive in the sterling bloc, and sterling bloc exports that competed with German goods in other markets now had a significant price advantage. Thus, although the depreciation of the pound eased Germany's debt burden somewhat, it also diminished Germany's exports, making it more difficult for the country to earn the foreign exchange it needed to service those debts.

The depreciation of the British pound gave Germany another opportunity to consider a devaluation. However, the government remained committed to keeping inflation and expectations of inflation in check. The day after Britain's abandonment of gold, German officials ruled out any devaluation. Instead, because the mark was now overvalued, Germany had to use ever tighter exchange controls to prop up the mark. In November 1931, to conserve the precious foreign exchange earned through exports, Germany introduced a scheme to ration the spending of foreign exchange. Accredited importers were allocated 75 percent of the foreign exchange that they had used during a base period of July 1930 to June 1931. To further limit spending on imports, in January 1932 this foreign exchange quota was supplemented with a tariff surcharge on goods from countries that did not have a commercial treaty with Germany.

These measures failed to stem the loss of foreign exchange reserves, forcing the government to economize further. As shown in figure 2.1, the allocation was slashed to 55 percent in April 1932. In May it was reduced to 50 percent, where it remained for nearly two years. The shrinking allocation of foreign exchange for imports did not require as drastic a contraction in imports as it appears in the figure because import prices continued to fall. But there is little doubt that exchange controls and foreign exchange rationing significantly reduced spending on imports.

Unfortunately, this was an imperfect way of managing Germany's balance-of-payments difficulties. It did not solve the problem of the mark's overvaluation, which made the country's exports more expensive for foreign consumers and foreign goods cheaper for domestic consumers. Germany's

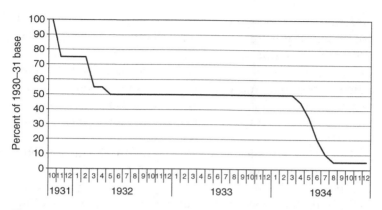

Figure 2.1
Germany's allocation of foreign exchange for imports. *Source:* Ellis (1941, 183, 204) and James (1986, 388).

exports had to be subsidized and its imports had to be deliberately squeezed to keep the two roughly in balance. The rationing of foreign exchange helped restrict imports, while indirect subsidies helped support exports. Exporters were encouraged to use their foreign exchange earnings to buy up heavily discounted German bonds in London and New York. The Reichsbank would then repurchase this debt in domestic currency at something close to face value. The German exporter gained, and the country's foreign currency debt was paid down at less than face value. The program amounted to a 10 percent subsidy on total exports, but as it was applied selectively, the effective subsidy sometimes reached 20 to 30 percent on specific products (James 1986, 392; Tooze 2007, 78).

Of course, instead of the complex web of import controls and implicit export subsidies, a devaluation could have solved the problem of the overvalued mark. But the German government not only refused to change the exchange rate, it continued to pursue a policy of deflation. The government hoped that by reducing domestic wages and prices faster than other countries, the overvaluation of the mark might be remedied. This would improve the balance of trade and stabilize the country's gold and foreign exchange reserves. Unfortunately, deflation simply plunged the economy even deeper into the depression.

Thus, the decision not to devalue the mark was a fateful one. The decision was made because of the ever present fear of inflation and worries about its impact on foreign currency debts. With the hyperinflation of the early 1920s burned into public memory, the government feared that any significant increase in domestic prices would lead to political chaos and social unrest. By imposing exchange controls, Germany effectively went off the gold standard, but it did not use that opportunity to pursue a reflationary monetary policy. As Feinstein, Temin, and Toniolo (2008, 99–100) note:

In one of the great ironies of history, Chancellor Brüning did not take advantage of this independence of international constraints by expanding. He continued to contract as if Germany were still on the gold standard. Brüning's actions at this time are vivid testimony to the power of ideology: leaders like Brüning felt compelled to cling to orthodoxy even as the world economy collapsed. He continued to advocate gold-standard policies after abandoning the gold standard itself. He ruined the German economy—and destroyed German democracy—in the effort to show once and for all that Germany could not pay reparations.

Because the economy continued to deteriorate, the mainstream political parties lost support among voters. This allowed the Nazi Party to gain parliamentary seats in the July 1932 election, and in January 1933, Adolph Hitler was invited to become chancellor.

Today, many economists have suggested that reflation would have promoted an economic recovery and spared Germany the fate of Nazi rule, but that is not how it was seen at the time. "The decision not to depart from parity against gold was in 1932 understood was a kind of bulwark against Hitler," writes Borchardt (1984, 497), "whereas today there are authors who consider this same decision as one of the principal causes of the national catastrophe from which Hitler emerged as the winner."

In April 1933, the United States left the gold standard and allowed the dollar to fall in value. As when Britain had done so, the impact on Germany was mixed. While Germany's dollar-denominated debts became easier to service, the depreciation of the dollar made it even harder for Germany to earn those dollars through exports. By 1934, the mark was estimated to have been overvalued by about 40 percent. As a result, Germany's merchandise trade balance shifted from surplus into deficit.

The efforts to reduce imports and stimulate exports failed to improve the country's balance-of-payments position. The Reichsbank's foreign exchange reserves plummeted in early 1934 as speculation about a possible devaluation put additional pressure on the mark. By June the central bank had barely enough reserves to cover a week's worth of imports. The foreign exchange crisis made it increasingly difficult to import raw materials, which threatened to shut down key industries and stop any economic recovery. Again, Germany confronted a choice between devaluation and even more restrictive exchange controls. Again, it never seriously considered a devaluation because it was considered too risky for a country with large foreign debts and small foreign exchange reserves. And so exchange controls were tightened even more. The allocation given to importers was slashed to 45 percent in

March 1934, 35 percent in April, 25 percent in May, and then down to 5 percent in August.

In June, Germany declared a moratorium on all debt repayments, thereby suspending payments on all foreign currency debts. The rationing of foreign exchange was abandoned and the government began doling out foreign exchange on daily basis. Blaming the Allies for the reparations burden they had put on Germany, Reichsbank president Hjalmar Schacht (1934, 4) lamented the country's fate:

> The present position of Germany has become so acute that she is stripped of all gold and foreign exchange reserves, and is obligated to reduce her own imports. . . . Possibly a people of seventy millions in the heart of Europe, with a high standard of living and a powerful demand for raw materials, must withdraw from the commerce of the world. So much economic nonsense has already been caused through politics that this folly may also be perpetrated.

In September 1934, Schacht announced a "New Plan" that gave the government complete control over all international transactions. All spending of foreign exchange, which had been rationed for private use, now had to be approved by the government. No importer could obtain foreign exchange unless the request was approved by a control board that examined criteria such as the desirability of the imports, the price of the imports, and the method of payment. Each proposed import transaction was carefully scrutinized by one of sixteen different control boards that determined whether purchases were permissible or not. This created a huge bureaucracy with 18,000 employees working on currency control matters (Tooze 2007, 94). The government had complete discretion over whether to approve, modify, or disapprove the importer's request (Ellis 1941, 211). The regulations required oversight of exports as well, since exports might be priced in a way to avoid exchange control restrictions.

In essence, the government established authoritarian control over the foreign trade sector of the economy. Permission to import goods was granted only if the goods served, directly or indirectly, the goals established by the government. "The measures taken in response to the foreign exchange crisis of 1934 laid the organizational foundation for the management of the Nazi economy for years to come," Tooze (2007, 93) notes. The objective was not only to eliminate Germany's trade deficit but to alter the structure of trade. In particular, the Nazi regime sought to shift the composition of imports away from consumer goods toward the industrial goods needed for rearmament. It attempted to do this by increasing exports and reducing imports of finished goods. The regime also aimed to reduce imports from European industrial countries, where the bitterness of the problems with reparations still stung, and increase exports to countries supplying Germany with raw materials, particularly those in southeastern Europe.

When Germany refused to honor its debts, Britain and others initially threatened trade sanctions. However, Germany soon reached bilateral agreements with these countries under which it would resume the servicing of debts. For example, Britain and Germany concluded a payments agreement in which 55 percent of Germany's earnings of sterling would be spent on British goods, 10 percent used to service Germany's debts, and the remainder free for disposal. Similar payments agreements were reached with other Western countries.

But Germany also sought a more extreme way of conserving scarce foreign exchange: altogether avoiding its use in international transactions. This was done through the use of bilateral clearing arrangements. Such clearing arrangements were very complex. In a typical example, say between Germany and Hungary, no exchange of gold or hard currency

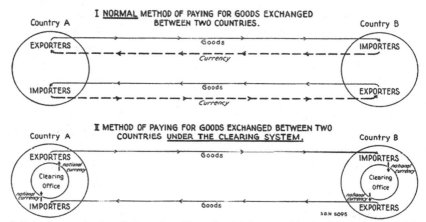

I. Under the normal system, the two reciprocal flows of goods between countries A and B are accompanied by two opposite flows of currency representing the value of the goods and proceeding from the importers of each country to the exporters of the other.

II. Under the clearing system, only the two flows of goods remain ; the external flows of currency are abolished. Inside each of the countries, a flow of the national currency proceeds from importers to the clearing office and from the clearing office to exporters.

Figure 2.2
Payments under the clearing system. *Source:* League of Nations (1935, 28).

was involved at all. Germany's exports to Hungary would be paid for in domestic currency by the Reichsbank, not by the Hungarian importer. Similarly, Germany's imports from Hungary would be paid by the central bank of Hungary in domestic currency.[13] As figure 2.2 shows, clearing arrangements bypassed the multilateral payments system of convertible currencies and pushed trade in a bilateral direction so that it could be conducted without foreign exchange at all.

The purpose of clearing arrangements was simply to allow Germany to engage in trade despite the severe shortage

---

13. However, because the mark was overvalued at its official parity, German goods were relatively expensive to purchase, leaving Hungary with a bilateral trade surplus. The imbalance would not be settled with gold or

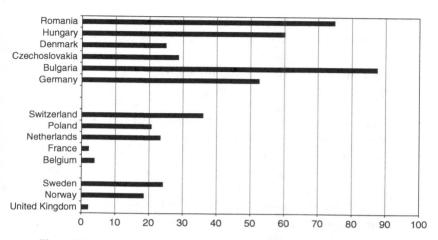

Figure 2.3
Percentage of imports through clearing arrangements, 1937. *Source:* Gordon
(1941, 133).

of foreign exchange resulting from its overvalued currency.
Clearing arrangements were an outgrowth of exchange controls and inconvertible currencies; it was a means of both ef-
fecting payment and influencing direction of trade. Germany
used clearing arrangements to conduct trade with other
exchange control countries in southeastern Europe, such
as Austria, Hungary, Bulgaria, Greece, Yugoslavia, and Romania. Figure 2.3 shows the percentage of imports financed

foreign exchange, since that would go against the purpose of the clearing
arrangement. The imbalance could have been eliminated with a change
in the official exchange rate, or with bilateral tariffs or import quotas, but
that was also ruled out. Instead, Hungary accumulated credits—"blocked
marks"—with the Reichsbank, with which it could buy German goods. There
was no automatic means to eliminate the blocked marks. One alternative was
to simply allow the foreign country to continue accumulating credits. Hungary's central bank could pay out domestic currency at a fixed rate for the
blocked marks. This would be like extending credit to Germany by domestic

through clearing arrangements for fourteen countries. By the mid-1930s, 60 percent of Germany's trade was conducted through clearing agreements and another 20 percent was conducted through barter arrangements. This left only 20 percent to be determined on a competitive basis using foreign exchange (League of Nations 1938, 196). The high percentages for Romania, Bulgaria, and Switzerland reflect the fact that Germany was one of their main trading partners. That is, these smaller countries did not seek clearing arrangements but rather conducted a large proportion of their trade with Germany, which did use them.

Because of the bureaucratic complexity involved, clearing arrangements were an inefficient way of promoting trade, and in fact they constrained it. The League of Nations (1935, 15) was highly critical of them, noting that "the general tendency of clearing agreements is constantly to reduce the volume and value of international trade and to subject it to forms of restraint that necessarily hamper its development."

Germany's new trade and payments policies are often said to have created an informal empire in southeastern Europe, allowing it to exploit the region through monopolistic practices. Yet recent research has cast doubt on this interpretation. The terms of trade did not move in Germany's favor; it purchased imports from southeastern Europe at a higher price than could be obtained elsewhere, and its export performance remained poor. Instead, the whole convoluted system reflected Germany's financial weakness, and its contorted efforts to get around the mark's overvaluation led to burdensome exchange transactions (Neal 1979; Ritschl 2001).

---

monetary expansion. However, other countries, such as Romania, did not want to monetize the difference at the official exchange rate and instead allowed the blocked marks to accumulate. This depressed the implicit value of the blocked mark, which fell below the official rate (Neal 1979).

Germany's trade policy in the 1930s is also sometimes described as autarkic. But as Tooze (2007, 86) explains, it was in fact a "selective policy of disengagement directed above all against the United States, the British Empire and, to a lesser degree, France," countries to which Germany owed money. Through a policy of import substitution, it reduced imports of finished manufactured goods from Western Europe and expanded imports of raw materials from Central and Eastern Europe. Germany used clearing arrangements to reorient its trade away from the Allies (which required hard currency) and toward countries in southeastern Europe (which also used exchange controls). Thus, clearing arrangements were consistent with this facet of the New Plan.

During the 1930s, trade relations with Germany's largest creditor, the United States, were severely strained. They especially deteriorated after Hitler came to power. In October 1934, Germany withdrew from the 1923 Treaty of Trade and Friendship with the United States, and the United States retaliated by withdrawing most-favored-nation (MFN) status from German goods. To conserve its scarce earnings of dollars, Germany sought to replace its purchases of U.S. raw materials with goods from Latin America. For example, Brazilian cotton was an adequate substitute for American cotton, and so the two countries developed bilateral trade on nondollar terms. The New Plan and bilateral clearings were a complete anathema to the American emphasis on promoting market forces in world trade through the nondiscriminatory multilateralism of the Reciprocal Trade Agreements program.

Other countries in southeastern Europe followed Germany's path, although the policies were not as extreme. They refused to change their gold parity out of fear that it would lead to monetary excess and excessive inflation, and instead imposed exchange controls. Because of their overvalued currencies, they suffered from chronic balance-of-payments problems. They also reached payments agreements with Western European countries; for example, one negotiated by Hungary and Switzerland provided that one-third of the receipts from Hungary's exports to Switzerland would be credited to repaying outstanding debts.

In sum, because Germany refused to alter the official exchange rate, it remained committed to a system of complete government control over all foreign exchange transactions. These exchange control restrictions became Germany's trade policy, but the controls involved much greater governmental interference with trade than just tariffs or quotas. Germany's core problem was its severe payments difficulties.[14] Because of its exceptional fear of inflation and struggles to service its foreign debt, Germany was unable to consider what almost every other European country eventually did, namely, a devaluation of its currency against gold. The exchange control countries provide an extreme example of how the breakdown of the multilateral payments system led to severe problems in sustaining international trade.

The United States

The interaction between exchange rate policy and trade policy is also seen in the case of the United States. In fact, the policy dilemma—a fixed gold parity with protectionism, or currency depreciation with freer trade—was essentially presented to the electorate in the 1932 presidential election.

---

14. Territorial expansion also helped support Germany's balance of payments: the annexation of Austria and the takeover of Czechoslovakia in 1938 roughly doubled Germany's gold and foreign exchange reserves, the sale of which in 1938 and 1939 allowed the country to run a large trade deficit in 1938 without financial difficulty (Ritschl 2001, 330; Tooze 2007, 246).

Voters chose the second option because the American economy had suffered long enough under the first.

As we have seen, the United States entered the Great Depression with the gold standard as its monetary system and having enacted the Smoot-Hawley Tariff Act in June 1930. During the European financial crisis in the fall of 1931, the United States was able to withstand the pressure and stay on the gold standard. The credibility of the exchange rate peg was backed by a large quantity of gold reserves. Still, the United States lost a sizable fraction of its reserves, and the Federal Reserve was forced to raise interest rates sharply to persuade foreign investors not to sell their dollars in exchange for gold. Unfortunately, the higher interest rates pushed a weak economy into the depths of the Great Depression.

Having successfully maintained the gold parity in late 1931, the United States saw its import tariffs rise over the next two years. Congress took no additional legislative action to impose new trade barriers after the Smoot-Hawley tariff, but because of continued price deflation, the ad valorem rates of the many specific duties in the tariff code increased significantly. Consequently, the average tariff on dutiable imports rose from 53 percent in 1931 to 59 percent in 1932 (Irwin 1998).

The failure to impose new protectionist measures during the Great Depression can be attributed to divided government, something unique to nonparliamentary political systems. Divided government refers to a situation in which the executive and legislative branches of government are controlled by different political parties. The two main political parties proposed resolving the open-economy policy dilemma differently: the Republicans favored the gold standard and high trade barriers, while the Democrats favored low trade barriers and were less committed to gold as a monetary standard.[15]

After the midterm elections in November 1930, the low-tariff Democrats captured the House of Representatives, while the Republicans remained in control of the Senate and the presidency. Because of the policy disagreement between the two parties, Congress would be unable to pass any new trade policy measures. For example, after the British pound fell against the dollar in late 1931, Republicans wanted to take action to stop imports from countries with depreciated currencies, just as many other countries that remained on the gold standard had done. In 1932, a number of bills were introduced in Congress to impose countervailing duties on imports coming from such countries (Scroggs 1933). However, Democrats were opposed to higher tariffs and used their control of the House to block any consideration of these proposals.

The future of U.S. policy was decided in the presidential election of 1932. The Republican incumbent, Herbert Hoover, firmly defended high tariffs, such as those in the Smoot-Hawley Act, and advocated staying on the gold standard. As late as February 1933, Hoover argued in favor of a worldwide restoration of the gold standard and against further currency depreciations, which he suggested would lead to "a world economic war, with the certainty that it lead to complete destruction, both at home and abroad" (Temin and Wigmore 1990, 488). His Democratic rival, Franklin Roosevelt, criticized high tariffs and did not rule out a possible departure from the gold standard.

---

15. These political preferences date back to the late nineteenth century; recall William Jennings Bryan's famous "cross of gold" speech in 1896. See Frieden (1997).

Roosevelt was elected president, and the Democrats gained control of both the House and Senate. A month before his inauguration, the president-elect hinted that he wanted to end the deflation and increase farm and industrial prices by shifting to a more inflationary monetary policy. This sparked rampant speculation that the United States would leave the gold standard and triggered a run on the dollar. The Federal Reserve lost large amounts of gold reserves, leading to a banking crisis just as Roosevelt took office in early March 1933 (Wigmore 1987).

In April 1933, Roosevelt announced his support for legislation that would allow him to set the dollar price of gold. The legislation, which soon passed Congress, effectively gave him the power to devalue the dollar if he wanted to. At the same time, he issued an executive order prohibiting the export of gold, which effectively ended the convertibility of dollars into gold. By these measures, President Roosevelt took the country off the gold standard. As a result, the dollar fell sharply on foreign exchange markets. By July, the dollar had declined 13 percent against the Canadian dollar and between 30 and 45 percent against other major currencies (Temin and Wigmore 1990, 489; Hallwood, Macdonald, and Marsh 2000).

The dollar's depreciation had an immediate impact on U.S. foreign trade. With the cheaper dollar making American products less expensive to foreign consumers, the volume of U.S. exports surged 40 percent between the first and fourth quarters of 1933. Although the depreciation of the dollar made foreign goods more expensive to American consumers, however, imports did not fall. Instead, the abandonment of the gold standard allowed interest rates to fall and fueled expectations of higher prices, all of which led to an immediate economic revival. This rebound helped push up import volume by 23 percent over the same period.

The key benefit that came with the abandonment of the gold standard was that it allowed the Federal Reserve to ease monetary policy. This meant that it could now adjust interest rates in line with domestic economic conditions, not simply to defend the dollar's gold parity. Abandoning the gold standard and the easing of monetary conditions had an immediate effect on the U.S. economy. The four-year deflation of prices stopped and prices began to rise slowly. Industrial production began to increase and unemployment began to fall. As Temin and Wigmore (1990, 485) put it, "The devaluation of the dollar was the single biggest signal that the deflationary policies implied by adherence to the gold standard had been abandoned . . . the devaluation of April–July 1933 was the proximate cause of the [economic] recovery."

More than any other element of the New Deal, the abandonment of the gold standard and the relaxation of monetary policy were critical to the subsequent economic recovery. (In fact, other New Deal programs, such as the National Industrial Recovery Act, actually hindered the recovery.) After nearly four years of grueling depression, the Roosevelt administration liked the improved economic outlook that came with the dollar's fall. Therefore, when world leaders at the World Economic Conference in July 1933 sought coordinated efforts to restore exchange rate stability, Roosevelt torpedoed the effort. "The sound internal economic situation of a nation is a greater factor in its wellbeing than the price of its currency," he explained. Roosevelt's statement, which undermined the entire premise of the meeting, reflected a change in priorities: the fixed exchange rate under the gold standard would be given up for an independent monetary policy geared toward domestic price stability.

The abandonment of the gold standard also paved the way for a scaling back of America's protectionist trade policy.

During the presidential election campaign, Roosevelt had been a critic of the Smoot-Hawley Tariff Act. He and his advisers, particularly Secretary of State Cordell Hull, saw it as fostering protectionism abroad and encouraging discrimination against the United States. Although a unilateral tariff reduction was ruled out, in March 1934 Roosevelt formally requested that Congress grant the executive branch the authority to enter into agreements with other countries to reduce tariffs.[16] As he explained, "a full and permanent domestic recovery depends in part upon a revived and strengthened international trade and that American exports cannot be permanently increased without a corresponding increase in imports." Noting that other countries were actively engaged in negotiating trade agreements that excluded the United States, Roosevelt argued that

if American agricultural and industrial interests are to retain their deserved place in [world] trade, the American government must be in a position to bargain for that place with other governments by rapid and decisive negotiation. . . . If [the government] is not in a position at a given moment rapidly to alter the terms on which it is willing to deal with other countries, it cannot adequately protect its trade against discriminations and against bargains injurious to its interests. (Tasca 1938, 300)

Administration officials repeatedly stressed that the United States was losing its fair share of world trade because of foreign trade restrictions and discriminatory measures against it.

In June 1934, about a year after the United States left the gold standard and allowed the dollar to depreciate, Congress passed the Reciprocal Trade Agreements Act (RTAA).

16. In April 1933, Roosevelt announced his intention to request authority from Congress to negotiate tariff-reduction agreements with other countries, but this was postponed to give Congress the time to pass more pressing New Deal legislation.

This legislation allowed the president to reduce U.S. import duties by up to 50 percent in trade agreements that included the unconditional MFN clause. The RTAA proved to be one of the most important institutional changes in the history of U.S. trade policy, and it paved the way for future tariff reductions.[17] By 1940, the United States had signed trade agreements with twenty-one nations that accounted for over 60 percent of U.S. trade.

The RTAA was a modest success in reducing U.S. tariffs during the 1930s. A report by the Tariff Commission calculated the duties that would have been collected in 1934 had the tariff resulting from the first thirteen country agreements implemented by 1936 been in effect. It found that the average U.S. tariff on dutiable imports would have fallen from 46.7 percent to 40.7 percent, a six percentage point drop, or a 13 percent cut, bringing the average tariff back to where it had been prior to the enactment of the Smoot-Hawley duties (Tasca 1938, 188). And in fact, the U.S. tariff fell by much more than this amount owing to the rise in import prices, which reduced the ad valorem equivalent of specific duties (Irwin 1998). Thus, it could be said that the tariffs negotiated under the authority of the RTAA effectively reversed the Smoot-Hawley increase, with the added advantage that the agreements also reduced foreign tariffs on U.S. exports.

Although the RTAA was only a modest step toward freer trade, the key point is that trade liberalization did not occur until after the United States left the gold standard and allowed its currency to depreciate. The United States resolved

---

17. See Haggard (1988), Bailey, Goldstein, and Weingast (1997), and Irwin and Kroszner (1999), and Hiscox (1999). Of course, U.S. trade policy was not completely liberal during the 1930s, as agricultural price support programs enacted as part of the New Deal led to the imposition of import quotas on selected goods.

the policy dilemma in a clean way: fixed exchange rates under the gold standard went hand-in-hand with protectionism, while abandoning the exchange rate peg permitted more open trade policies.

France and the Gold Bloc

France and the gold bloc—Belgium, Italy, the Netherlands, Poland, and Switzerland—managed to avoid any serious speculative attacks against their currency during the financial turmoil of 1931. As a result of their substantial gold reserves, their commitment to the gold standard was unquestioned, and their currencies were viewed as safe havens. The Bank of France actually gained gold reserves in 1931, as other currencies were buffeted by the financial chaos around the world. Thus, France and the gold bloc did not at this time have to consider the possibility of allowing their currency to depreciate or imposing exchange controls. They did not suffer an immediate crisis in the form of a rapid outflow of gold reserves that had forced other countries to choose one policy or the other.

However, after the depreciation of the sterling bloc currencies, the gold bloc currencies became overvalued. Although their ample gold reserves made any immediate change in the gold parity unnecessary, over time the overvalued currencies began to change their balance-of-payments situation: exports became more expensive to foreign consumers and began to flounder, while foreign imports became much cheaper and hence more attractive. To counteract growing trade deficits, which would lead to a gradual erosion of their gold reserves, the gold bloc countries began to restrict imports through higher tariffs and new quantitative restrictions.

As the largest country in the gold bloc, France set the trend for commercial policy. France could not easily raise tariffs to offset the impact of the franc's overvaluation because it was party to many commercial agreements, concluded in the late 1920s, that locked in about 70 percent of the rates in its tariff code. Although French and gold bloc tariffs did increase during this period, such agreements were an obstacle to any general increase in tariff rates (Haight 1935, 6).

However, these agreements did not prevent France from imposing quantitative restrictions on imports.[18] Introduced in mid-1931, quotas were initially used to reduce imports of agricultural goods. After the sterling bloc countries left the gold standard, France expanded its use of import quotas to cover manufactured goods as well. "In the ten months after July 1931, there were 61 decrees covering more than 1,100 items of the tariff schedule, or about one-seventh of the whole," Haight (1935, 13) reports. At first, the quotas were supposed to be temporary, and in fact their duration was fixed. They were initially justified to prevent a surge of imports as a result of the depreciation of other currencies. The quotas soon became a more permanent feature of French commercial policy, however, and were justified as necessary to improve the balance of trade and defend the currency.

Unlike a uniform increase in tariffs or a depreciation in a country's currency, import quotas were inherently arbitrary in their application. The permissible amount of imports could change from month to month, sometimes being relaxed, sometimes becoming more restrictive. The allocation of the quota rights across countries could also change

18. For example, the Franco-German treaty of 1927 allowed both sides to take any measure regarding exports or imports necessary for protecting vital economic interests under extraordinary or abnormal circumstances (Haight 1935, 7–8). "These measures may only be taken in case of exceptional necessity and must not constitute an arbitrary means of protecting national production."

arbitrarily without much notice. So while French officials insisted that the quantitative measures were nondiscriminatory, it was almost impossible to make a quota regime compatible with MFN treatment. This led to many trade disputes. For example, Britain believed it had received an unusually small quota on some of its goods and imposed surcharges on French goods. Similarly, Germany objected to the French restrictions on its exports and retaliated by erecting similar barriers on French products (Haight 1941, 174). Many of the "trade wars" of the 1930s consisted of spats about trade restrictions on specific products that led to a cycle of retaliation and counterretaliation.

Other gold bloc countries adopted import quotas as well. The Netherlands and Switzerland used them mainly to limit imports of manufactured goods, while Belgium used them to block imports of agricultural goods. Like France, they also took the opportunity to increase tariffs on imports. These small open economies had traditionally kept trade barriers low and had limited government intervention. Yet exchange rate policy could not be made in isolation, and the constraints imposed by fixed exchange rates had spillover effects for other economic policies. For example, the refusal to change the exchange rate parity led to other government interventions in the economy. Straumann (2010, 127–128, 132) notes that "instead of suspending the gold standard, business leaders and their political allies were demanding a series of state subsidies and protectionist measures despite their strongly held belief in a free-market economy." Protectionism was therefore "a consequence of a monetary strategy that was endorsed by all major parties, business associations, and unions."

The overvaluation of the gold bloc currencies intensified in 1933 when the United States left the gold standard and the dollar depreciated in value. After the U.S. decision, France, Belgium, Italy, the Netherlands, Poland, and Switzerland were the only major countries that remained committed to the gold standard. In a joint statement during the World Economic Conference of June 1933, the countries called the gold standard "essential for the economic and financial recovery of the world" (Straumann 2010, 129). They strongly supported the conference, which was held with the goal of stabilizing exchange rates and seeing whether fixed rates could be restored under the gold standard. However, as we have seen, the Roosevelt administration, seeing the benefits of the depreciation of the dollar, refused to support these goals and the conference ended in failure.

With their overvalued currencies eventually leading to a loss of gold reserves, the gold bloc countries thought they could deflate their way out of their growing balance-of-payments difficulties. Instead of changing the gold parity, they would simply reduce domestic wages and prices and thereby restore balance-of-payments equilibrium. These countries resisted a devaluation because their leaders feared it would lead to inflation that would be difficult to control (Straumann 2010, 132). In their view, the gold parity ensured monetary discipline. Exchange controls were an option, but not in France and Switzerland. Like Britain, they were international banking centers where businesses depended on convertible currencies and international capital flows, making resort to foreign exchange restrictions very costly.

Bertil Ohlin was acutely aware of the dilemma faced by the gold bloc. Ohlin correctly saw that the gold bloc had to realign its domestic costs, which were high relative to the rest of the world, either by deflation ("the adoption of radical remedies to force the entire levels of costs down" by 20 percent or more) or by "a suitable measure of devaluation."

To Ohlin, the choice between deflation and devaluation was a far-reaching one: "it is clearly a question of choosing between the one or the other alternative and of adopting the entire economic policy—even agricultural and foreign trade policy—to whichever one is chosen."

However, in a prescient article entitled "Can the Gold Bloc Learn from the Sterling Bloc's Experience?," Ohlin (1936, 62) was skeptical that deflation would work: "The hopes entertained in various quarters within the gold bloc of being able, as a result of an early rise in prices and wages in sterling countries and America, to evade the difficult choice between heavy general reduction in wages and a devaluation of the currency are hardly likely therefore to prove justified." To Ohlin, the choice was between a policy of contraction or a policy of expansion. Without explicitly endorsing a devaluation, Ohlin made clear where his sympathies lay: "Experience has proved that we must abandon our old preconceived ideas that there is only one kind of monetary system, only one kind of budgetary policy, etc; and in fact only one kind of economic policy that is sound and proper in all situations, while all measures of any other kind are taboo."

In choosing deflation rather than devaluation, the gold bloc countries essentially committed themselves to a regime of trade restrictions through import quotas. Yet trade controls could not solve the underlying problem, an overvalued currency. Rather, it only eased to a slight extent the deflationary path these countries had to follow. This path failed to reduce the costs of production in the gold bloc relative to other countries, and the gold bloc remained mired in a prolonged slump. This led to increasing public frustration with the state of the economy. In the end, every member of the gold bloc eventually left the gold standard; the democratic countries opted for

devaluation, while the authoritarian countries opted for exchange controls. In May 1934, Italy imposed capital controls.
In March 1935, Belgium devalued its currency. In April 1936,
Poland imposed exchange controls. And in September 1936,
the three remaining countries—France, the Netherlands, and
Switzerland—either devalued or allowed their currencies to
depreciate.

Belgium was the first key gold bloc country to defect. The
deflation it endured had been more severe than in France.
Also, as a smaller economy, it was much more dependent on
exports than France, and its exports had been crushed by the
overvaluation of its currency. After the dollar left gold, more
and more Belgian economists and public officials began ad-
vocating devaluation as a solution to the country's woes. A
moderate banking crisis and a political crisis in 1934 led to
a weakening of the reserve position of the National Bank of
Belgium. The Belgian government vowed to defend the franc.
But in early 1935, with gold losses accelerating and political
resistance to deflation increasing, the government flinched
and threatened to impose exchange controls unless France,
its largest export market, liberalized its import quotas on
Belgian goods. France refused. Meanwhile, the threat of exchange controls spooked investors, and they began dumping
their holdings of the Belgian franc. In March 1935 the Belgian
government collapsed, and the new government almost immediately devalued the currency by about 28 percent (Mouré
1991, 115–116).

Poland also suffered severe deflation and collapsing industrial production during the Great Depression. Despite
its dismal economic performance, Poland stayed on the gold
standard for a long period of time because, unlike democracies such as Belgium, its authoritarian regime could safely
ignore the economic suffering without fear of the political

consequences.[19] In addition, having experienced a hyperinflation in 1923 and another bout of inflation in 1925–1926, Poland valued the monetary stability that it believed the gold standard provided. Furthermore, national security concerns, namely, a fear of Germany, made it want to remain a member of the gold bloc in order to preserve its close economic and financial ties to France. However, political events soon forced Poland off the gold standard. Germany's remilitarization of the Rhineland led to fears of war and triggered speculation against the zloty. In April 1936, after losing a substantial amount of its gold and foreign exchange reserves, Poland introduced exchange controls.

Despite its increasing economic problems, France also wanted to stay on the gold standard, and the government dismissed any change as inconceivable. However, as in Belgium, the wisdom of this view soon became the subject of intense national debate. In 1934 the former finance minister, Paul Reynaud, previously a strong advocate of wage and price deflation, began to call attention to the alternative of devaluation. His argument consisted of three points. First, the disparity in prices between France and the rest of the world was the source of its balance-of-payments and economic problems. Second, the price disparity could be remedied either by deflation in France, or by inflation elsewhere, or by a change in the exchange rate. Finally, he insisted that the increasing economic costs of deflation had to be recognized, as well as the success that other countries had achieved with devaluation (Mouré 1991, 204). Despite Reynaud's observations, many more opponents to devaluation wanted to stay the course with the gold standard.

---

19. Wolf (2007) finds that, had Poland not been an authoritarian regime, it most likely would have gone off the gold standard in September 1931.

The growing public impatience with the ongoing economic stagnation led to the election of the socialist Popular Front in May 1936. The new government had gained power on the promise of increased government spending. It rejected devaluation as strongly as its predecessor but recognized that increased spending would put pressure on the balance of payments. In lieu of a devaluation, therefore, it hinted at the need for capital controls. The expectation that such controls might be implemented put the franc under intensified selling pressure on foreign exchange markets. France now faced the choice of following either the German path of using exchange controls and extending government control over all foreign exchange transactions or the British model of allowing its currency to depreciate. Arguing with Prime Minister Léon Blum, Reynaud argued that a refusal to devalue would necessarily lead to exchange controls and "economic fascism" (Mouré 1991, 242). France, he insisted, must choose to remain economically aligned with the Western democracies instead of authoritarian governments in Germany and Central Europe.

Such arguments, along with the declining public support for continued monetary deflation, weakened the government's resolve to defend the gold parity. Eventually, the government agreed to allow the franc to fall, but only in an orderly fashion. Consultations with Britain and the United States provided assurance that they would support France's decision to go off the gold standard. In September 1936, France and the Netherlands allowed their currencies to float on the foreign exchange market, while Switzerland devalued its currency against gold.

The other gold bloc countries were also reluctant to change their gold parity. In examining the political debate in

Switzerland over the issue, Bordo, Helbling, and James (2007) found a "surprisingly broad consensus for maintenance of the existing parity," despite the economic difficulties that entailed. The main argument against devaluation was that it would harm the nation's banking sector. Financial interests were strongly opposed to any change in the exchange rate on the grounds that such a move would diminish the country's reputation for monetary probity. Surprisingly, even Swiss exporters opposed devaluation; they feared it would increase the cost of raw materials and other imported inputs.[20] In addition, Swiss exports were largely directed toward Germany and Central Europe, both of which had exchange and administrative controls on trade, so it did not anticipate that devaluation would bring any great improvement in export competitiveness. Even domestic farmers, who were already protected by import duties and quotas, opposed devaluation.

Therefore, with great reluctance, Switzerland followed France in devaluing its currency. The only silver lining for conservative interests was that devaluation headed off more radical changes in economic policy—for example, extensive government intervention, or even socialist policies—that were brewing if the economic situation did not improve.

According to the trilemma hypothesis, once a country gives up its gold parity and allows its currency to depreciate, it should no longer need protectionist trade policies for balance-of-payments purposes. In fact, Ohlin (1936, 161) predicted that the gold bloc countries would "after devaluation find it less necessary to resort to import restrictions." And he was right: after the gold bloc countries devalued their

---

20. Switzerland exported specialty manufactured goods, not price-sensitive staple products, and so its firms did not believe that a lower price would stimulate foreign sales.

currencies and their economic recovery began, they started to dismantle some of their trade barriers. As the League of Nations (1942a, 85) noted, "Before the end of October 1936, tariff reductions and/or quota relaxations had been announced in France, Switzerland, the Netherlands, Italy, Czechoslovakia, and Latvia." For example, the month after its currency fell in value, France reduced its tariffs on raw materials by 20 percent and its tariffs on manufactured goods by 15–17 percent (Haight 1941, 181). It also suspended quotas on about a hundred products, covering about a quarter of its imports. In addition, Switzerland slashed many of its import tariffs by more than 50 percent.

Thus, the final breakup of the gold standard in 1936 was a welcome development from the standpoint of world trade policy. By relaxing the gold constraint and allowing countries to pursue more expansionary monetary policies, the pressure to maintain restrictive trade policies was relieved. The League of Nations' *World Economic Surveys* for 1936/37 and 1937/38 took note of a slight "net movement" toward the liberalization of world trade as a result of these developments.

Conclusion

This chapter has provided narrative evidence from Britain and the sterling bloc, Germany and the exchange control group, the United States, and France and the gold bloc to see how they resolved the policy trilemma. The general conclusion tends to support the view that policymakers were faced with trade-offs among these objectives and that a reluctance to devalue one's currency led to significant restrictions on trade and payments. The gold standard mentality was so strong that policymakers were willing to embrace the heresy of higher tariffs and protectionism rather than depart from the gold standard. In making these choices, each country was constrained by its history, both in terms of its recent past—the extent to which monetary instability in the 1920s bred a deep fear of inflation—and its position on international financial markets. The next chapter examines empirical measures of trade and exchange rate policy to see if they support the narrative evidence as well.

3 Trade Restrictions and Exchange Rate Adjustment: Choice and Consequences

This chapter presents economic data from the 1930s to address three issues. First, we examine the impact of protectionism on world trade in the 1930s based on a counterfactual assessment of how much trade would have fallen had there been no change in trade policy. Several different calculations suggest that about half of the 25 percent decline in world trade was due to higher trade barriers. Second, we analyze several measures of trade policy to see if the pattern is consistent with the trilemma interpretation. The trilemma leads us to expect that countries allowing their currencies to depreciate would not adopt protectionist measures to the same extent as countries maintaining their currency at the gold parity. Empirical measures of trade policy in the 1930s—tariffs, import quotas, and exchange controls—generally support this prediction. Third, we examine the broad macroeconomic ramifications of the exchange rate choices made during the Great Depression. Exchange rate changes and import restrictions are similar in the sense that a devaluation is equivalent to an import tariff and an export subsidy. In practice, however, the two policies are quite different in their effects on macroeconomic performance and international trade.

The Impact of Protectionism on World Trade

World trade declined precipitously during the Great Depression. Between 1929 and 1933, the value of world trade fell by an astounding 65 percent in gold-dollar terms. The famous downward spiral of world trade, shown in figure 3.1, is a striking graphical depiction of this contraction. As the world slid into the depths of the Depression, the year-over-year value of world trade fell every month for more than four years.

Of course, the nominal value of trade fell partly because prices were falling. But even after controlling for deflation, trade fell significantly. Between 1929 and 1932, the volume of world trade shrank by 25 percent. The decline was not symmetric across all categories of traded goods. Trade in manufactured goods collapsed, falling 41 percent between 1929 and 1932. This is not entirely unexpected because trade in durable goods is typically very sensitive to economic fluctuations. However, trade in manufactured goods failed to rebound; by the end of the decade, it still had not returned to its 1929 peak, something that is anomalous. Trade in raw materials dropped 19 percent between 1929 and 1932 but recovered by the end of the decade. Trade in agricultural goods fell the least, just 11 percent over the same period, but remained depressed through the decade (League of Nations 1939c, 61). Of course, the prices of agricultural goods and raw materials fell much more than the prices of manufactured goods. This produced a sharp deterioration in the terms of trade for developing countries and aggravated the economic downturn of countries in Asia and Latin America.

Figure 3.2 shows the path of world trade and world real GDP from 1925 to 1938. While trade grew slightly faster than GDP in the 1920s, the drop in trade was much greater than the decline in GDP during the Great Depression. Whereas GDP

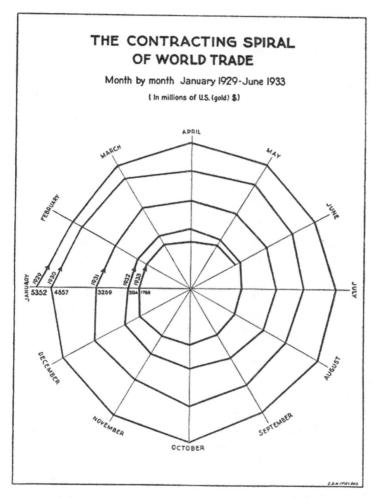

Figure 3.1
The declining spiral of world trade, 1929–1933. *Source:* League of Nations (1933).

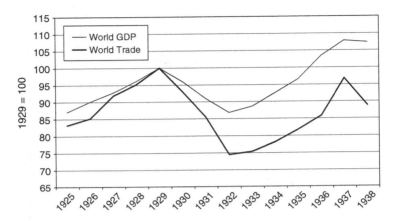

Figure 3.2
World trade and world GDP, 1925–1938. *Source:* World trade (volume):
League of Nations (1939c, 62). World real GDP: Maddison (2010).

fell 13 percent between 1929 and 1932, trade fell 25 percent.
The decline in trade was particularly sharp in 1932, the year
after the 1931 financial crisis. The volume of trade fell 16 percent from the third quarter of 1931, just prior to these events,
to the third quarter of 1932 (League of Nations 1939c, 62). This
outcome is consistent with the proliferation of restrictions on
international trade and payments that emerged after Britain
abandoned the gold standard.

After 1932, the world economic recovery was steady, but
not robust. World GDP did not surpass its 1929 peak until
1936. In a marked break from the usual pattern following an
economic downturn, the recovery in trade was much weaker
than that of income. By the end of the decade, the volume of
world trade was still below its 1929 peak.

The decline in the import-to-GDP ratio of various countries illustrates the more rapid fall in trade relative to GDP
during this period. As figure 3.3 shows, the ratio of imports

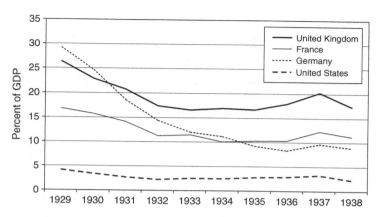

Figure 3.3
Imports as a share of GDP, 1929–1938. *Source:* Imports and nominal GDP: data for Germany from Ritschl (2004), for the United Kingdom and France from Mitchell (2007), and for the United States from U.S. Department of Commerce (1976).

to GDP fell for all major countries between 1929 and 1932, even in the period preceding the dramatic increase in trade barriers. (This is one reason why most domestic producers could not demand protection on the grounds that imports were capturing a larger share of the domestic market.) While the ratio stabilized in Britain once that country's currency depreciated, the ratios continued to fall in France and Germany, where they did not level off until much later in the decade. Germany experienced an enormous compression of imports; its import-to-GDP ratio fell from nearly 30 percent in 1929 to less than 10 percent by 1935.

What was the contribution of protectionism to the collapse of world trade in the early 1930s? Did the 25 percent reduction in world trade simply reflect the 13 percent decline in world income, or were trade barriers also a contributing factor?

Table 3.1
Decomposition of Change in Volume of World Trade, 1929–1937

	Change in trade volume (%)	Due to		
		Change in GDP (%)	Change in tariffs (%)	Change in non-tariff barriers (%)
1929–1932	−25	−11	−10	−4
1932–1935	+6	+8	−1	−1
1935–1937	+23	+14	+5	+4

Source: Derived from Madsen (2001).

Madsen (2001) provides the best estimate of the impact of protectionism on world trade in the 1930s. He estimates import demand equations for the leading countries and decomposes the changes in trade into changes in income (GDP), import tariffs, and non-tariff barriers (captured by a dummy variable). According to his results, summarized in table 3.1, more than half of the decline in trade between 1929 and 1932, about 55 percent, can be attributed to higher trade barriers. Additional trade barriers stifled the growth of trade between 1932 and 1935. From 1935 to 1937, a modest reduction in trade barriers contributed to the expansion of trade.

Another indirect way of determining the contribution of protectionism to the trade collapse is to focus on the discrepancy between world production of manufactured goods and world trade in manufactured goods. Figure 3.4 presents data on the annual changes in the trade and production of manufactured goods. During the 1920s, with the exception of one year, trade grew more rapidly than production. Of course, trade also fell more than production in the early 1930s, with 1932 being an unusually bad year. The recovery period is particularly striking: starting in 1933, production

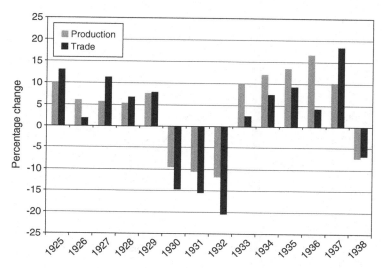

Figure 3.4
World trade and production of manufactured goods, 1925–1938. *Source:* United Nations (1962).

rebounded strongly, but trade did not. In fact, the recovery in trade lagged far behind that of production. By 1938, world trade in manufactured goods was still well below its 1929 peak, whereas world production exceeded its 1929 peak by a significant margin.

Using these data, we can speculate about the path that world trade in manufactured goods might have taken during the 1930s if the actual relationship between trade and production in the 1920s had continued to hold. We can estimate a simple regression for the short sample period of 1921–1929 and then use it to forecast trade based on actual changes in production during the 1930s. The specification is

$$\Delta \log (\text{trade}) = \alpha + \beta \, \Delta \log (\text{production}) + \varepsilon.$$

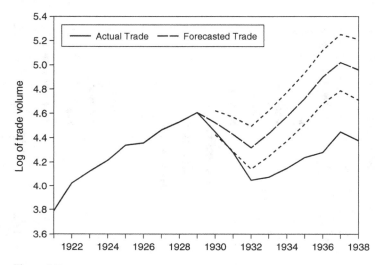

Figure 3.5
Actual and predicted trade in manufactured goods, 1921–1938

The estimated coefficient β is 1.03 (with a standard error of 0.14) and the regression's R^2 is 0.72.

Figure 3.5 depicts the actual path of trade and the out-of-sample forecast of trade based on this regression (including ± two standard errors around the forecast). The forecast indicates that, if the relationship between world production and trade in the 1920s had continued into the 1930s, we would have expected world trade in manufactured goods to have fallen 25 percent between 1929 and 1932. In fact, world trade in manufactured goods fell 43 percent during this period. From this we can say that about 60 percent of the decline in trade can be attributed to falling production and 40 percent to other factors. Higher trade barriers were likely to have been responsible for much of the 40 percent.

As figure 3.5 shows, the forecast not only understates the decline in world trade in 1930–1932 but vastly overstates the recovery. Based on the relationship between production and trade in manufactured goods during the 1920s, world trade volume in 1938 should have been 42 percent above the 1929 peak, rather than 20 percent below the peak. In other words, trade would have been about 80 percent greater than it actually was. Clearly, something was seriously awry in the behavior of trade in the 1930s. This is indirect evidence that trade policies are likely to have suppressed the growth of trade during this period.

The same is true for agriculture. Between 1920 and 1929, world production in agricultural goods grew 37 percent, while agricultural trade grew 61 percent. Even though world agricultural production was more than 10 percent higher in 1938 than it had been in 1929, world agricultural trade remained 10 percent below the 1929 peak.[1] Unfortunately, because the relationship between production and trade in agricultural goods is not as stable as that for manufactured goods, it is not possible to estimate a statistical relationship that would help explain the breakdown in the 1930s. By most accounts, however, protectionist measures imposed on agricultural trade were particularly onerous.

Surprisingly few studies have investigated the impact of protectionism on world trade in the 1930s. Estevadeordal, Frantz, and Taylor (2003) present a decomposition to explain the rise and fall of world trade between 1870 and 1939, as measured by the world's trade-to-GDP ratio. Using a gravity model of bilateral trade, they attribute changes in the

---

1. The agricultural trade data come from Aparicio, Pinilla, and Serrano (2008) and the agricultural production data come from the League of Nations (1939c, 15).

trade-to-GDP ratio to three factors: payments frictions (the number of countries adhering to the gold standard), policy frictions (average tariffs), and transport frictions (shipping costs). Between 1929 and 1938, the world's trade-to-GDP ratio fell from 15 percent to 9 percent. Of that decline, they attribute 29 percent to the collapse of the gold standard, 14 percent to higher tariffs, 27 percent to higher transport costs, and the remainder to other factors.

This decomposition implies that trade restrictions were not necessarily the most important factor behind the decline in the world's trade-to-GDP ratio. But there are two reasons to treat this finding with skepticism. First, the decline in trade attributed to policy frictions vastly understates the effect of trade barriers. As we have seen, import tariffs were just the tip of the iceberg when it came to trade-restricting policy interventions, and they were probably not the most significant impediments to trade during the period. The extensive use of non-tariff barriers to trade, particularly import quotas and exchange controls, are not captured by their measure. By understating the impact of policy frictions, the empirical model probably overstates the role of other factors in reducing trade.

Second, Estevadeordal, Frantz, and Taylor use a standard ocean shipping freight rate index (the Isserlis series) to measure transportation costs. According to their calculations, real freight rates increased in the early 1930s, and this operated as a significant brake on world trade. Given the substantial excess capacity that existed in the world's maritime shipping industry at this time, a finding of rising transportation costs is odd. Subsequent studies of freight rates, notably that by Shah Mohammed and Williamson (2004), find that real freight rates fell in the early 1930s and rose again only as the world economy began to recover. Thus, the decomposition exercise may be based on misleading transport cost data. By attributing a large amount of the decline in world trade to higher transportation costs, the authors' calculations probably understate the detrimental role played by trade barriers.

Jacks, Meissner, and Novy (2009) provide another perspective on interwar trade by focusing on the evolution of trade costs. Trade costs include all frictions that inhibit exchange between markets, including not just tariffs and transportation costs but insurance and distribution costs, information and contract enforcement costs, legal and regulatory costs, other government policies, and so forth. These costs cannot be measured directly but can be inferred from gravity equations using bilateral trade data. They find that average trade costs fell 7 percent between 1921 and 1929 but rose 21 percentage points between 1929 and 1932, the most dramatic increase over their entire sample from 1870 to 2000. While growth in output should have led to an 88 percent increase in trade between 1921 and 1939, according to their results, an increase in trade costs reduced trade by 87 percent. In other words, rising trade costs completely offset other forces working to expand trade during this period.

Unfortunately, the question of why those costs rose so sharply in the early 1930s is left unanswered. They do not have direct measures of trade policy, so they are unable to determine the precise role played by barriers created by government policy. They attribute changes in trade costs to distance between countries, fixed exchange rates, a common language, the existence of a shared border, and membership in a colonial empire. Most of these factors did not change in the early 1930s, so the increase in trade costs is largely unexplained, but it is entirely consistent with a sharp rise in protectionism.

Looking at price differentials for the same good in different countries is a more direct way of measuring the frictions that inhibit exchange between markets. Hynes, Jacks, and O'Rourke (2009) document commodity price disintegration during the interwar period, showing that price gaps between major markets increased for virtually every type of agricultural good. They find no evidence that the widening of the price gaps was the result of increasing transport costs. Instead, they suggest that trade policies were responsible for the segmentation of commodity markets, although they do not have direct evidence of this.

Finally, there is one major question that is often implicitly discussed but almost never directly confronted. That question is whether the destruction of trade as a result of protectionist trade barriers intensified the Great Depression. Falling income clearly led to falling trade, but did the additional reduction in trade due to protectionism lead to an additional fall in national income? Certainly, many contemporaries believed that, by reducing world trade, the spread of trade restrictions exacerbated the Depression. In fact, this is actually an extremely difficult question to answer because it is hard to determine the precise impact of trade on a country's national income.

From a national income accounting perspective, an equal reduction in exports and imports has no measured impact on GDP; only an increase in net exports will increase the calculation of GDP. But this is a very poor way of assessing trade's contribution to the economy. Trade is usually thought to increase national income through increased productivity.[2] In this way, more trade may lead to greater income by increasing some of the components of the national income accounts, such as consumption or investment. But this makes the measurement of trade's contribution to higher income very

---

2. Trade increases productivity either through greater product-market competition or the diffusion of technology. For a discussion of these channels, see Irwin (2009).

difficult to trace. Not only are these productivity-related factors difficult to detect in the national income accounts, they tend to operate over the medium and long run rather than at a business cycle frequency.

Furthermore, from the perspective of trade theory, higher trade barriers may reduce trade and diminish economic welfare, but they do not necessarily reduce national income as measured by government statisticians. Numerical estimates of deadweight losses can approximate the decline in welfare that comes from the imposition of trade barriers, but these deadweight losses tend to be a small fraction of GDP. Even in the 1930s such deadweight losses are calculated to be very small in comparison to the decline in national income (Irwin 2010b). As James Tobin (1977, 468) famously quipped: "It takes a heap of Harberger triangles to fill an Okun's gap."[3]

One crude way of addressing the question of whether protectionism contributed to the Great Depression is to rely on estimates that quantify the effect of an exogenous change in trade on income. Until Frankel and Romer (1999), this had never been done. They overcame the simultaneity problem—that higher income leads to more trade, and more trade leads to higher incomes—by drawing on the fact that distance between countries is an important determinant of bilateral trade, but is independent of income. Frankel and Romer isolated the non-income, geographically determined component of trade and found, not surprisingly, that more trade is systematically related to higher income.

Feyrer (2009) provides the best and most recent estimate of the elasticity of income with respect to exogenous changes in trade and finds that it is about 0.3; that is, a 10 percent exogenous increase in trade leads to a 3 percent increase in income.

---

3. The Harberger triangle is a measure of the deadweight loss, while Okun's gap refers to the difference between potential and actual GDP.

As noted earlier, the world trade-to-GDP ratio was 15 percent in 1929, and a 25 percent drop in trade—holding income constant—would reduce it to 11 percent. A reduction of four percentage points in the trade share implies that world income fell by about 1 percent (4 × 0.3 = 1.2) at a time when world GDP fell about 13 percent. Therefore, one might cautiously speculate that something close to one-tenth of the decline in world income during the Great Depression was due to the policy-induced reduction in trade. Although it is hard to put much faith in this number, it does suggest that the destructive trade policies of the period could have played a significant role in intensifying the economic contraction.

To conclude, declining output explains much of the decline in world trade, but not all of it. Something else was going on, and the likeliest candidate is government policy: protectionism in the form of higher trade barriers.

The Trilemma and Trade Barriers

So far we have described the protectionist response during the 1930s and examined its impact on world trade, but we have not looked at quantitative measures of trade barriers during the period. Trade policies are notoriously difficult to measure, and empirical measures of such policies from the 1930s are scarce. Yet rough numerical indicators of import tariffs, import quotas, and exchange controls exist, and bringing this data together should give us a sense of how much these trade barriers rose during this period. More important, the cross-country pattern of the use of these trade policy instruments should provide some evidence as to whether the trilemma interpretation is valid or not.[4]

---

4. This section draws extensively on Eichengreen and Irwin (2010).

The most basic trade policy instrument is the import tariff. A simple measure of the average tariff on imports can be calculated by dividing customs revenue by the value of imports. This measure is subject to numerous qualifications, but it is still a useful indicator of the average height of a country's tariffs.[5]

The three panels in figure 3.6 present the average tariff for leading members of the sterling bloc countries, the exchange control group, and the gold bloc countries.[6] Most countries increased their tariffs in the early 1930s, but large countries appear to have increased tariffs more than small countries. The most pronounced increases in duties were in Britain, France, Germany, and Italy, which were less dependent on trade than smaller countries.

It also appears that the sterling bloc countries with depreciated currencies increased their tariffs the least. The tariffs of the sterling bloc were relatively low and stable through the 1930s. Britain is a big outlier in this group, for reasons discussed in chapter 2, and the increase in fiscal duties by Norway is also evident. But the tariffs of the other Nordic countries and in Japan increased very little.[7] By contrast, the exchange control group and the gold bloc, both of which maintained their gold parity, seem to have increased their tariffs the most. In the gold bloc, rates of import duty roughly doubled. France and Belgium saw the largest tariff increases, while the rise was more muted in the Netherlands

5. See Irwin (2010b) on alternative tariff measures for the United States.
6. These data are available in Clemens and Williamson (2004). They are based on data on customs revenue and the value of imports presented in the historical statistical yearbooks compiled by Brian R. Mitchell.
7. Although Denmark allowed its currency to depreciate and did not increase tariffs, it also imposed exchange controls. However, the tariff may not have been the binding constraint on trade.

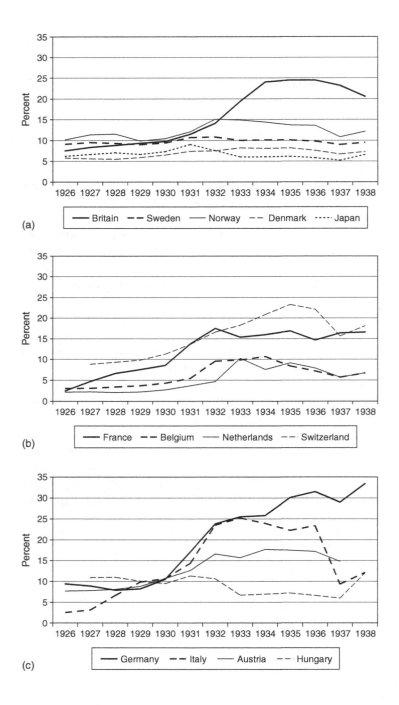

(a)

Legend: Britain — Sweden — — Norway — Denmark — — Japan ·····

(b)

Legend: France — Belgium — — Netherlands — Switzerland — —

(c)

Legend: Germany — Italy — — Austria — Hungary — —

and Switzerland. With the exception of Hungary, tariffs also increased among the exchange control countries. The change in tariffs might be expected to have been more varied in exchange control countries. By their nature, exchange controls are a way of reducing imports, making additional tariffs unnecessary. Yet even if an exchange control country did not need higher duties to reduce imports, such duties could still be a valuable revenue-raising device for governments. For example, tariffs in exchange control countries, particularly Germany and Italy, rose sharply in the early 1930s.

A comparison of Nordic countries (Denmark, Finland, Norway, and Sweden) and the Low Countries (Belgium and the Netherlands) is informative because of their similarity: all were small, open economies that historically imposed minimal taxes on imports. Yet their policies diverged sharply during this period: the Low Countries maintained their gold parity and increased their tariffs much more than the Nordic countries, which allowed their currencies to depreciate. This pattern is consistent with the trilemma.

Figure 3.7 provides a sharper test of the trilemma implication that exchange rate depreciation and higher tariffs were alternatives. The scatterplot shows changes in tariffs and exchange rates for various countries between 1929 and 1935.[8]

◄ Figure 3.6
Average import tariffs. (a) Sterling bloc countries. (b) Gold bloc countries. (c) Exchange control countries. Source: Clemens and Williamson (2004).

8. The measure of the change in the tariff is $\log(1 + \tau_{1935}) - \log(1 + \tau_{1929})$. The percentage change in the tariff rate itself would be misleading because going from a 1 percent duty to a 2 percent duty on imports doubles the tariff rate with little impact on trade, whereas going from a 10 percent to a 15 percent tariff, while only a 50 percent increase in duties, has a more substantial impact on imports.

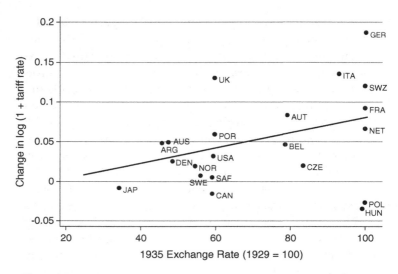

Figure 3.7
Change in average tariff and exchange rate, 1929–1935. *Source:* Eichengreen and Irwin (2010).

The year 1929 is the pre-Depression business cycle peak for most countries, while the year 1935 sits between the trough of the Depression and the gold bloc's departure from the gold standard. The figure provides clear evidence of a pattern between the two: the regression line indicates that, for the most part, countries that allowed their currency to depreciate had smaller increases in tariffs. Britain is an outlier from the general relationship, as are Hungary and Poland, which probably used exchange controls rather than tariffs to reduce imports. In sum, there seems to be a fairly strong relationship between a country's exchange rate policy and its decision to impose higher tariffs in the early 1930s.[9]

9. Eichengreen and Irwin (2010) provide additional checks on the robustness of this relationship and find that it continues to hold even with a larger

There is an alternative hypothesis: perhaps a country's decision to increase its tariffs was driven more by the severity of the Depression than by its choice of exchange rate policy. For example, it would be logical to assume that countries suffering from the biggest contractions in their output would increase their tariffs more than others. Yet, as figure 3.8 shows, between 1929 and 1935, there is no correlation between the change in a country's GDP and the change in its tariff.[10] The change in a country's exchange rate has a much stronger relationship to the change in the country's tariffs than the change in its GDP. There is a straightforward explanation for this finding. As noted earlier, imports are particularly sensitive to changes in domestic income and fell much faster than income in the early 1930s. Producers suffered greatly during the Great Depression, but not because of greater competition from imports. Most firms could not point to a rising tide of imports against which they needed protection.

Similarly, there is no correlation between high unemployment and a change in the tariff.[11] This is shown in figure 3.9, using unemployment data from 1933, the peak year of unemployment in most countries. The same is true with respect to the change in the unemployment rate, which controls for the different initial level of unemployment across countries.

In sum, the evidence on changes in exchange rates and tariffs in the early 1930s is consistent with the trilemma interpretation. Countries that failed to change their gold parity

---

sample of developing countries and after controlling for other factors, including the endogeneity of the exchange rate decision and changes in wholesale prices, which might influence the ad valorem equivalent of specific duties.

10. This lack of association does not depend on the specific year for the change in GDP; it also holds in other years, such as 1933, the trough of the Great Depression for most countries.

11. Historical unemployment data are unavailable for many countries, which limits the sample size.

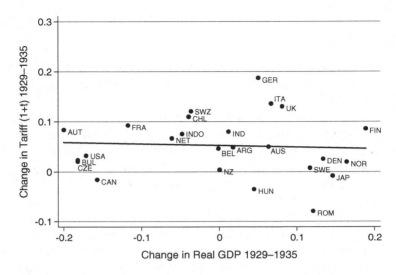

Figure 3.8
Change in average tariff and real GDP, 1929–1935. *Source:* Tariff data, from
Clemens and Williamson (2004) data. Real GDP data from Maddison (2010).

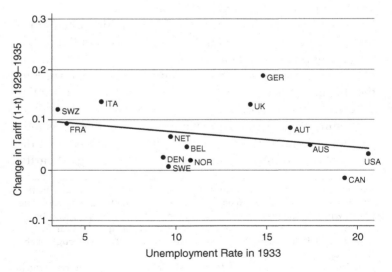

Figure 3.9
Change in average tariff and the unemployment rate. *Source:* Tariff data, see
footnote 52. Unemployment data from Grytten (2008).

tended to increase their tariffs more than countries that allowed their currency to depreciate. Meanwhile, countries that suffered the greatest reduction in income or the greatest increase in unemployment did not change their tariffs any more than countries that suffered less during the period.

Import Quotas

Data on the use of import quotas are very scarce for this period. However, the League of Nations reported the share of imports covered by quantitative restrictions and licenses for a few countries in 1937. Unfortunately, the restrictiveness on the quotas is unknown; that is, we do not know their implicit tariff equivalent or how much they reduced trade. However, information on the share of imports restricted by quotas does reveal how extensively they were used.

Figure 3.10 shows the relationship between the share of imports affected by import quotas in 1937 and the change in the exchange rate between 1929 and 1935. (The fact that there are no data on import quotas in 1929 is not a problem because quotas were rarely used at that time; see Gordon [1941, 243].) The relationship is unmistakable: countries that maintained their gold parity, such as France and Switzerland, made much more extensive use of import quotas than countries that allowed their currencies to depreciate, such as Britain and Sweden. The gold bloc countries used import quotas on about 50–60 percent of their imports, whereas the sterling group used them on only 5–10 percent of their imports. Exchange control countries are not represented in the League's sample. They did not resort to quantitative trade measures, presumably because the discretionary allocation of foreign exchange gave them control over the amount of imports allowed in any particular category of good.

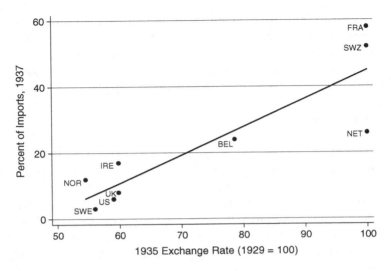

Figure 3.10
Share of imports covered by quantitative restrictions, 1937. *Source:* League of
Nations (1939a, 189) and Whittlesey (1937).

As in the case of tariffs, the use of quotas during the 1930s
is uncorrelated with the change in a country's real GDP. Once
again, exchange rate policy appears to be the key to understanding the pattern of import restrictions across countries.
This would not have surprised Bertil Ohlin. As he wrote:

Countries that have maintained parity with gold have been obliged
to protect themselves against low-priced exports from countries
with a depreciated currency. The latter's level of general costs . . .
has been reduced in terms of gold by 40–60 percent, whereas the
former have not succeeded in lowering theirs more than twenty percent or so. Under these circumstances most sterling countries have
succeeded in carrying on business without any appreciable quantitative trade restrictions, except as regards agriculture. . . . Until the
relation of the cost levels in different countries has become more or

less 'normalized' it is not to be expected that the countries of the gold bloc will abandon their quantitative regulation of imports. (Ohlin 1935, 61)

Ohlin speculated that production costs in the gold bloc countries would have to fall 20–30 percent relative to those in the sterling bloc to restore balanced trade. He was rightly skeptical that they could rely on deflation, as opposed to an exchange rate change, to reduce their costs by such a large amount. As he predicted, once the gold bloc countries allowed their currencies to fall in value, they scaled back their use of quotas.

Exchange Controls and Clearing Arrangements

The final trade policy measure to be examined is exchange controls. As noted earlier, exchange controls are potentially much more restrictive than either tariffs or quotas because they allow the government to determine exactly how much spending on imports will be permitted. As we saw in chapter 2, for example, after Germany imposed exchange restrictions in 1931, the government squeezed imports by reducing the amount of foreign exchange allocated to the purchase of foreign goods.

Unfortunately, information on the rationing of foreign exchange by country is not readily available. Nor can we measure the "tariff equivalent" of exchange controls, or have something like the coverage ratio. We know only which countries had exchange controls and which did not. Exchange controls were mainly used by Germany and countries in Central Europe. No member of the sterling bloc or gold bloc employed them for more than short periods of time during a crisis situation.

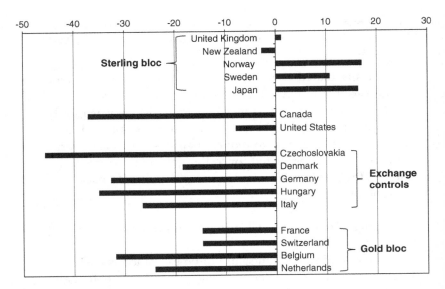

Figure 3.11
Change in volume of imports, 1929–1935. *Source:* League of Nations (1939a).

Because there are no quantitative measures that indicate how much exchange controls actually restricted international trade, their impact must be inferred from trade data itself. Figure 3.11 presents the change in the volume of imports for various countries, by group, between 1929 and 1935. It shows that, despite the depreciation of their currencies, imports by the sterling group countries were generally greater in 1935 than they were in 1929. By contrast, imports were significantly lower in exchange control and gold bloc countries.

While the figure is striking, the interpretation is not straightforward. Did exchange control countries import less because such controls reduced imports more than other countries or because their economies experienced a greater

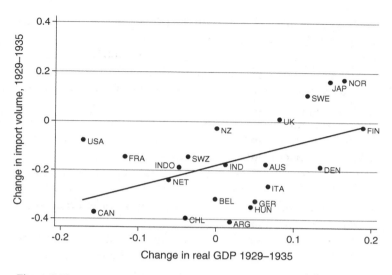

Figure 3.12
Change in import volume and real GDP, 1929–1935. *Source:* League of Nations (1939a) and Maddison (2010).

decline during the Depression? Figure 3.12 shows the change in real imports and the change in real GDP over the same period. The regression line shows the average relationship between the change in imports and the change in GDP. Notably, every single exchange control country is below the line. In a regression of the change in real imports on the change in real GDP and using a dummy variable for exchange control countries, Eichengreen and Irwin (2010) find that real imports were about 23 percent lower in exchange control countries compared to others. In other words, even when controlling for the change in their income, we can say that exchange control countries imported significantly less than other countries. This finding is consistent with the view that such controls had an especially restrictive effect on imports. Bhagwati (1978) discusses the distortions that come with exchange controls in general. Wei and Zhang (2007) examine the recent experience with exchange controls and confirm that they are among the most trade-destructive forms of government policy.

In sum, the use of protectionist trade measures in the early 1930s shows some discernible patterns. Countries that allowed their currencies to depreciate did not resort to restrictive trade policies—import tariffs, import quotas, and exchange controls—nearly as much as other countries that maintained their gold parity. These findings offer broad support for the trilemma interpretation of events.

A final implication of the trilemma is that countries that changed their gold parity after 1931 would then be free to dismantle some of these protectionist barriers. While there is no direct quantitative evidence on this point, chapter 2 described how the United States and France were able to move toward trade liberalization after their currencies depreciated. The United States began a program to reduce tariffs in bilateral trade agreements the year after the dollar depreciated, and France abolished many of its quotas about a month after the franc depreciated. By contrast, Germany and the exchange control countries never officially allowed their currency to depreciate relative to gold. Because they maintained their gold parity throughout the decade, they never liberalized their exchange control regimes and continued to suppress spending on imported goods.

Exchange Rates and Economic Performance

In the 1930s, a country's exchange rate policy affected not only its trade policy but also its international trade and macroeconomic performance. As we have seen, during the Great Depression, countries that maintained the gold parity could not undertake expansionary monetary policies. The only policy response available to them was import restrictions.

The trilemma framework itself implies nothing about whether a country should prefer exchange rate depreciation or import controls as an adjustment mechanism. In a narrow sense, the policy instruments are equivalent. As Keynes pointed out, a devaluation of (say) 10 percent is equivalent to a 10 percent import tariff combined with a 10 percent export subsidy (Chipman 2007). Both are expenditure-switching policies that shift spending from foreign goods to domestic goods. When a country is operating under a fixed exchange rate and has less than full employment, such policies have the potential to increase national output.

Of course, the effects of a depreciation and import controls are not equivalent when it comes to exports. Whereas a depreciation reduces the price of domestic goods to foreign consumers and thereby increases exports (hence the similarity to an export subsidy), import restrictions provide no benefit for, and may even reduce, exports. Therefore, a depreciation of one's currency should have a greater stimulative effect on an underemployed economy than import restrictions because it gives a boost to exports.

Yet currency depreciation and import restrictions have been criticized for being "beggar-my-neighbor" policies in which the benefit to the country imposing the measure comes by way of inflicting harm on other countries.[12] In her famous 1937 essay, "Beggar-My-Neighbor Remedies for Unemployment," Joan Robinson described four primary ways in which a country could increase its own output by reducing

---

12. The term "beggar my neighbor" comes from a nineteenth-century children's card game in England.

its imports from, and displacing the exports of, other countries: wage reductions, a currency depreciation, export subsidies, and import protection. Such policies would work only if few countries tried them; if every country tried to expand its economy by reducing imports, then every country's exports would fall because one country's imports are another country's exports. In the end, there would be no net stimulus to the economy, just a drop in world trade. As Robinson (1937, 227–228) concluded, "all [such] expedients are subject to the objection that they are calculated to promote retaliation; indeed this is the very nature of the beggar-my-neighbour game. Which expedient is the least dangerous from this point of view will depend upon general political considerations."

However, to lump exchange rate changes and import restrictions together in this manner takes a very narrow view of the matter. In practice, exchange rate changes and import restrictions are far from equivalent. The main advantage of a currency depreciation is not its expenditure-switching feature but the fact that it frees monetary policy from an exchange rate target and gives policymakers the discretion to use it to respond to a deflationary shock. An expansionary monetary policy can end deflation and reduce interest rates. This in turn will stimulate investment, all without having to worry about whether the exchange rate parity can be maintained. Thus, the combination of a devaluation and an expansionary monetary policy is expenditure switching and expenditure increasing. Furthermore, some of the benefits of increasing domestic expenditure spill over to other countries, possibly offsetting the adverse impact of expenditure switching on other countries. As a result, it is not clear that an exchange rate depreciation is always a beggar-my-neighbor policy.

By contrast, trade restrictions, such as import controls, are only expenditure switching. They are clearly a beggar-my-neighbor policy because they reduce the demand for other countries' exports. An increase in trade barriers does not give monetary policy much scope to be expenditure increasing, as we saw in the case of France and the gold bloc. Exchange controls provide monetary independence only to the extent that they move the country toward autarky, as we saw in the case of Germany. Thus, while trade restrictions might have some palliative effects for an economy with slack resources and a fixed exchange rate, such policies are relatively ineffective at providing a stimulus to the economy. As a result, import controls were not an effective substitute for monetary policy in promoting recovery from the Great Depression.

In an illuminating simulation, Foreman-Peck, Hughes-Hallett, and Ma (2007) looked at the impact of various policies to counter the Depression. They conclude:

> For all their damage to trade, trade policy instruments were not a powerful means of achieving national targets. Monetary and fiscal policies were far more effective. . . . The other two instruments—the discount rate and government expenditure—were clearly more potent and more appropriate to the three targets—output, prices and the current balance—than trade controls. (90)

They show that, in general, expenditure-switching policies are not as powerful as expenditure-increasing policy in alleviating a slump of the magnitude of the Great Depression.

There are other reasons why a depreciation of the exchange rate is fundamentally different from an increase in trade barriers. Robinson raised the issue of retaliation, which can undo any benefit that a country reaps from imposing import restrictions. If countries retaliate against trade partners that limit their imports, it can lead to a trade war. The result will be higher trade barriers all around and an overall reduction in world trade. Under these circumstances, no country will succeed in increasing net exports.

With a currency depreciation, the situation is different. If one country follows another country that has allowed its currency to fall on foreign exchange markets, there may be no change in bilateral exchange rates; both currencies will "depreciate" against each other, leaving the nominal exchange rate unchanged. But this is equivalent to a synchronized easing of monetary policy. In the early 1930s, when economies were plagued with deflation and high unemployment, such retaliatory depreciations could have led to an expansion of world demand and an increase in world trade free from trade barriers.

Thus, while superficially similar, exchange rate changes and trade policy interventions are fundamentally different. As Eichengreen and Sachs (1985, 945) note:

Protection, like devaluation, also is capable of exerting expansionary effects at home. But the adoption of tariffs by all countries (reducing producer prices and lowering output and employment) leaves everyone worse off; coordinated devaluation both at home and abroad together with accommodative monetary measures is likely to leave everyone better off. Too often competitive devaluation and tariff protection have been viewed as interchangeable. They are not.

And this is the way it played out during the Great Depression. In a classic paper on the macroeconomic consequences of the gold standard and the Great Depression, Eichengreen and Sachs (1985) showed that countries that went off the gold standard and allowed their currencies to depreciate were able to ease their monetary policies, reduce interest rates, stimulate domestic demand, and start the process of recovery. Campa (1990) found the same thing for Latin American countries, Temin and Wigmore (1990) for the United States, Bjørtvedt and

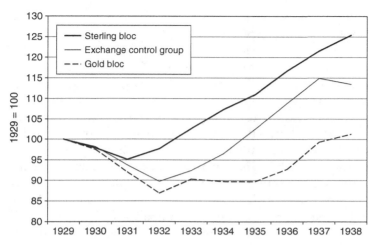

Figure 3.13
Real GDP by country group, 1929–1938. *Note:* The sterling bloc includes the United Kingdom, Sweden, Norway, Finland, Portugal, Ireland, and Japan. The exchange control group includes Germany, Austria, Bulgaria, Czechoslovakia, Hungary, Romania, Denmark, Italy, and Yugoslavia. The gold bloc includes France, Belgium, the Netherlands, Switzerland, and Poland. *Source:* Maddison (2010).

Venneslan (1999) for Norway, and Greasley and Oxley (2002) for New Zealand. Meanwhile, countries that remained on the gold standard suffered prolonged slumps until they, too, allowed the value of their currency to fall against gold.

Figure 3.13 illustrates this phenomenon by looking at the path of real GDP for the sterling bloc, the exchange control group, and the gold bloc. The sterling bloc countries began to recover in 1932, the year after their currencies were de-linked from gold. The exchange control group, which, despite maintaining the exchange rate parity, also went off the gold standard, began to recover in 1933. The gold bloc countries suffered an extended depression that did not begin to ease until 1936, when they left the gold standard and allowed their currencies to depreciate.[13]

Clearly, countries began to recover from the Great Depression only after they left the gold standard, either by allowing their currency to depreciate (sterling bloc) or by ending convertibility (exchange control group). The question is whether this renewed growth came at the expense of other countries and thereby constituted a beggar-my-neighbor policy.[14]

In standard Keynesian-type models, a depreciation increases the output of the country undertaking the depreciation, provided there is substantial unemployment in labor and capital. But what about its impact on other countries? A common way of assessing the impact on foreign output, and therefore judging whether the depreciation constitutes a beggar-my-neighbor policy, is to look at net exports. If the net export position of depreciating countries increased, then presumably it improved its trade balance (and hence, under this line of reasoning, its employment and output as well) at the expense of other countries.

Figure 3.14 shows the path of export and import volume for leading countries. Unfortunately, it is difficult to arrive at

13. In the case of Switzerland, even though major economic interest groups resisted a devaluation of the franc, the policy allowed the country to recover from its economic downturn. Share prices of bank stocks rose and the economy began to recover once the decision was made in September 1936. In a simulation, Bordo, Helbling, and James (2007) found that Swiss output would have been 18 percent higher in 1935 if the authorities had devalued the currency in 1931 instead of in 1936.

14. Bertil Ohlin (1935, 64) doubted that it was beneficial to other countries: "It is obvious that currency depreciation has been an essential condition of economic improvement in the sterling countries; which does not of course imply that this depreciation has been beneficial from the point of view of the world economy. . . . Its effect upon the economy of the gold countries has no doubt been unfavorable; it has intensified the deflationary pressure on their business life."

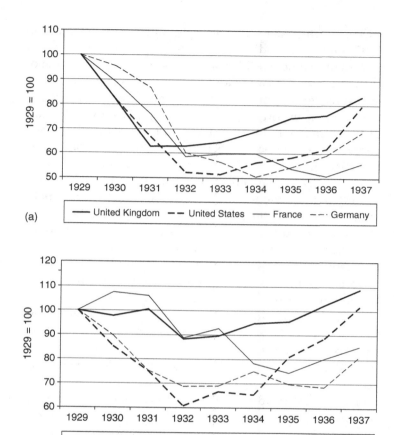

Figure 3.14
Volume of exports and imports, 1929–1937. *(a)* Export volume. *(b)* Import volume. *Source:* League of Nations (1939a).

a clear conclusion. In the case of Britain, exports stabilized in 1932, after the pound's depreciation. Although imports fell, it is difficult to know if this was because of the depreciation or the higher tariff. In a broader view of the matter, while British exports grew more rapidly than imports after the pound's depreciation, exports fell much more significantly at the start of the Depression. By 1937, the volume of Britain's imports exceeded its 1929 peak, whereas its exports were only at 85 percent of its 1929 level.

In the case of the United States, in 1933, the year of the devaluation, its import volume increased much more than its export volume. As in Britain, U.S. exports had fallen much more than imports between 1929 and 1932, and despite the full recovery of imports by the end of the decade, exports were still well below their 1929 peak. In the case of France, exports and imports began to grow only after the franc's depreciation in 1936.

Figure 3.15 provides a cleaner comparison by presenting the path of imports for two Scandinavian countries and the two Low Countries. These countries were all small, trade-dependent economies, but the Scandinavians allowed their currencies to depreciate in 1931, while the Low Countries stayed on the gold standard for at least four more years. While Scandinavian imports fell sharply in 1932, after the devaluation, a more expansionary monetary policy in 1932 and 1933 allowed the economic recovery to begin, and import volumes recovered rapidly. Meanwhile, the imports of the Low Countries remained depressed for the remainder of the decade. From these data it is apparent not only that countries with depreciated currencies were able to grow more rapidly but that this growth spilled over to the purchase of goods from trading partners.

Another way of judging whether the exchange rate depreciation had beggar-my-neighbor effects is by looking at the

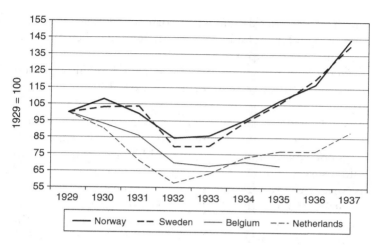

Figure 3.15
Import volume: Scandinavia and the low countries, 1929–1937. *Source:* League of Nations (1939a).

distribution of gold reserves. Eichengreen and Sachs (1986) show a sterilized devaluation—that is, when the gold backing given to a country's currency is adjusted in such a way that its overall level of reserves remains unchanged—is a beggar-my-neighbor policy. However, an unsterilized devaluation—that is, when a country adjusts domestic credit to maintain the ratio of gold backing to money in circulation—is not necessarily a beggar-my-neighbor policy. A rise in the gold reserves of nondevaluing countries is a necessary but not sufficient condition for output to increase in those countries. If the depreciating country is able to reduce interest rates and spur domestic demand while also losing gold reserves to other countries, that gold flow can ease monetary conditions in nondevaluing countries and stimulate economic activity there. Finally, they note, a "competitive" devaluation, in which all countries devalue their currency (that is, reduce the gold backing), is not a beggar-my-neighbor policy and succeeds in raising output in all countries.

The evidence suggests that the sterling bloc depreciation was unsterilized, and therefore it was probably not a beggar-my-neighbor policy. As noted, an increase in gold reserves by non-devaluing countries is a necessary but not a sufficient condition for the depreciation not to have been a beggar-my-neighbor policy. And, in fact, the gold bloc's share of world gold reserves continued to rise after the sterling bloc allowed its currencies to depreciate in late 1931. (The exchange control countries had already left the gold standard, and so their reserve position was less important.) Certainly for France, the main problem was not its lack of gold reserves but the fact that it was sterilizing its gold inflows so that they had little domestic effect. France's cover ratio (gold backing of domestic currency) was abnormally high, indicating that, regardless of what the sterling bloc did, it could have eased monetary policy. Still, Britain gained gold reserves in early 1932, but this may have been a recovery from the significant loss of gold it suffered in late 1931. Britain's share of world gold reserves was lower in December 1931 than it had been a year earlier, and it was lower still in December 1932. Sweden and Norway also lost gold reserves in the aftermath of their depreciation.

Thus, it does not appear that the depreciation of the sterling-bloc currencies attracted gold reserves at the expense of other countries and therefore exerted deflationary pressure on them. Given that the alternative was to maintain the gold parity and thereby continue to endure deflation and a prolonged economic slump, it is hard to see how this would have improved matters for other countries.

In sum, opting for an exchange rate adjustment not only avoided the destruction of trade that came with protection-

FRANCE. "AH! ZE POOR JOHN BULL, I AM SO SORREE FOR 'IM."
SAM: "WAAL, I'M NOT SO SURE THAT HE'S THE ONE WHO NEEDS THE SYMPATHY, BIG BOY!"

This cartoon by Sidney "George" Strube, published in the *Daily Express* on September 22, 1931, shows Britain on the road to trade recovery after having left the gold standard. Meanwhile, France and the United States are still weighed down by the gold standard. *Source:* British Cartoon Archive, University of Kent. Reproduced with permission from Express Syndication.

ism, it also had macroeconomic benefits in freeing up monetary policy and allowing the process of economic recovery to begin.

Trade Blocs and Currency Blocs

Another important trade policy development of the 1930s is the growth of preferential trade blocs. Countries not only adopted protectionist measures aimed at reducing imports, they also sought to redirect existing trade flows to preferred countries.

Trade preferences developed for a number of reasons. Historical ties encouraged special relationships to promote trade, as was the case with Britain and its former colonies. Deteriorating political relationships led to the use of discriminatory measures to reduce trade, such as the League of Nations' sanctions against Italy in response to its invasion of Ethiopia or U.S. efforts to discourage trade with Germany after the Nazi's seized power. Finally, payments agreements directed trade toward partners that did not require hard, convertible currencies as a medium of exchange and amounted to trade preferences, such as Germany's agreements with southeastern Europe. In addition, many of the trade measures used in the 1930s, such as import quotas and exchange controls, were inherently discriminatory in their application. Even tariffs could become discriminatory through refinements in the tariff schedule that privileged the products of favored nations.[15]

All of these policies distorted the existing multilateral pattern of world trade and payments and shifted trade into what seemed to be exclusive trade blocs. The rise of discriminatory trade policies in the 1930s created so many frictions and problems between countries that economists today, including Jagdish Bhagwati (2008), have drawn a parallel to current preferential trade agreements, warning that they give rise to discrimination that distorts world trade flows.

15. The classic example of having a de facto but not a de jure discriminatory tariff was the provision in the German tariff code, dating from 1902. To differentiate between cattle from Denmark and those from Austria and Switzerland, a provision related to "brown or dappled cows reared at a level of at least 300 metres above the sea and passing at least one month in every summer at a height of at least 800 metres."

Table 3.2
Changes in Intrabloc Trade, 1929–1938

Trade of	Share of	Imports (%)		Exports (%)	
		1929	1938	1929	1938
United Kingdom	British Commonwealth, colonies, protectorates	30	42	44	50
	Other countries of the sterling bloc	12	13	7	12
France	French colonies, protectorates, mandated territories	12	27	19	28
Belgium	Belgian Congo	4	8	3	2
Netherlands	Overseas territories	6	9	9	11
Portugal	Overseas territories	8	10	13	12
Italy	Colonies and Ethiopia	1	2	2	3
Japan	Korea, Formosa, Kwantung, Manchuria	20	41	24	55
Germany	Six countries of southeastern Europe	5	12	5	13
	Latin America	12	16	8	12

Note: Sterling bloc countries include Sweden, Norway, Finland, Denmark, Egypt, Estonia, Latvia, Portugal, Thailand, and Iraq. The six countries of southeastern Europe are Bulgaria, Greece, Hungary, Romania, Turkey, and Yugoslavia.
Source: League of Nations (1939b, 186).

Table 3.2 presents the shift in trade patterns that may have been a result of these policies. Most major European countries began to channel trade to their former colonies or current overseas territories.

In terms of tariff preferences, Britain made the most important change in policy and seems to have altered its trade pattern the most. At least since the mid-nineteenth century, Britain had been committed to nondiscriminatory free trade. As the country's commitment to free trade weakened during the Great Depression, so too did its commitment to nondiscrimination as a basis for its commercial policy. There had long been support in the Conservative Party for formalizing closer economic ties to its dominions around the world. At a conference in Ottawa in July and August 1932, Britain finally agreed to establish a system of imperial preferences. The products from the empire were also exempt from the General Tariff that Britain had imposed in early 1932.

The tariff preference that came out of the Ottawa conference put U.S. exporters at a significant cost disadvantage in selling into two markets that together took nearly a quarter of U.S. exports, Canada and the United Kingdom. Partly as a result of this discrimination, the U.S. share of British and Canadian imports declined noticeably during this period.[16] The American desire to eliminate discriminatory trade policies was as much a motivation for the formation of the GATT after World War II as the goal of reducing trade barriers.[17] In fact, a 1945 State Department document noted that the United States was "far more interested in the elimination or reduction of the bound margins of preference in favor of British countries than in [the] reduction of the United Kingdom's most-favored-foreign-nation tariffs" (Dűr 2010, 80).

Aside from the imperial preferences established by Britain and its empire, however, most of the "trade blocs" of

---

16. In 1929, Canada took 18 percent of U.S. exports, while Britain took 16 percent. In 1937, about half of British exports to and imports from the Commonwealth enjoyed preferences on the order of 20 percent, on average (Macdougall and Hutt 1954). Partly as a result of this discrimination, the U.S. share of Canada's imports fell from 69 percent in 1929 to 54 percent in 1933, while that of Britain rose from 15 percent to 24 percent (Hart 2002, 96). Similarly, from 1929 to 1934, the U.S. share of Britain's imports fell from 16 percent to 11 percent and was still at that low level in 1937, while the share of its former empire rose from 29 percent in 1931 to 39 percent in 1937 (Kottman 1968, 117).

17. See Irwin, Mavroidis, and Sykes (2008).

the period were rooted not so much in discriminatory tariff treatment as in quota allocations, clearing arrangements, payments deals, and currency linkages. One problem with interpreting the changes in the pattern of trade in table 3.2 is that many factors aside from trade preferences, such as currency ties and payments arrangements, were also an important determinant of trade flows. For example, did France start trading more with its colonies because of formal trade preferences or because they shared a common currency, and so trade flows between them were not affected by the overvaluation of the franc?

Such interpretive difficulties are especially significant in the case of Germany. Did trade between Germany and southeastern Europe expand because of formal trade preferences or because the clearing agreements encouraged trade among countries with nonconvertible currencies while the mark's overvaluation discouraged trade with other countries? Ritschl (2001) points out the problems in explaining the changing shares of trade for southeastern Europe, suggesting that the collapse of trade with Russia accounted for much of the change. In addition, some of Germany's increasing share of trade with southeastern Europe "was simply the reestablishment of older trading patterns that had been disrupted by the inflations and upheavals of the 1920s" (Feinstein, Temin, and Toniolo 2008, 154). It has been common to think about Germany fostering the reichsmark bloc—consisting of Bulgaria, Greece, Hungary, Romania, Turkey, and Yugoslavia—for the deliberate and nefarious purpose of commercial domination leading to military conquest. Yet as we have seen in chapter 2, the clearing arrangements did not represent German power and strength but its weakness and its inability to finance trade with other countries. Germany was unable to exploit these countries economically, and in fact, its terms of trade deteriorated as a result of these arrangements.[18]

These uncertainties suggest that a more systematic effort is needed to determine the impact of trade blocs and currency arrangements on the changing pattern of world trade at this time. It is helpful to recognize that the trade and currency blocs were not always overlapping. For example, although the sterling bloc and the imperial preferences overlapped to some extent, Denmark, Norway, Sweden, Portugal and others were part of the sterling bloc but did not receive trade preferences, and Canada and Honduras belonged to the Commonwealth but did not join the sterling bloc. This potentially allows us to identify the trade impact of each group.

Eichengreen and Irwin (1995) used a gravity model approach to examine whether trade and currency blocs were responsible for the changing patterns of world trade in the 1930s. They found that countries that were members of these various trade and currency blocs already traded intensively with others in 1928, with only marginal increases in bilateral trade in 1935. While they found that imperial preferences did increase intrabloc trade, there was little evidence that currency blocs significantly affected the pattern of trade. They concluded that "the tendency toward regionalization commonly ascribed to the formation of trade and currency blocs was already evident prior to the regional policy initiatives of the 1930s; to a considerable extent it is attributable to ongoing historical forces such as commercial

---

18. See Neal (1979), Milward (1981), Ritschl (2001), and Hedberg and Håkansson (2008). "From the moment Hitler became Chancellor any change of reintegrating Germany into an internationally-agreed payments system disappeared," Milward (1981, 397) notes. "The Reichsmark bloc, far from being a positive policy, was a desperately unsatisfactory attempt to maintain, at high international costs to the Germany economy, the absolute primacy of domestic economic policy."

and financial linkages between countries forged over many years."

Recent work has supported these conclusions. Wolf and Ritschl (2011) focus on the endogenous selection of countries into these trade and currency blocs. In particular, they find that membership in such arrangements is predicted by previous trade and political relationships. They conclude that, owing to this endogeneity, trade and currency blocs did not create much trade among the partner countriess. Similarly, Gowa and Hicks (2010) finds that trade blocs did not have a positive impact on bilateral trade flows and that such blocs did not lead to a significant fall-off in trade between member and nonmember states.

Thus, discriminatory trade practices proliferated in the interwar period, but—with the exception of Britain and its partners—the discrimination was probably rooted more in the breakdown of the multilateral payments system than in the spread of preferential trade agreements. Tariffs were just one of many types of trade interventions, and perhaps not the most significant of them. In addition, while discriminatory policies succeeded in shifting the pattern of trade, they may have been less important than might appear to be the case from table 3.2. Instead, the generalized rise in trade barriers that squeezed overall trade was a more important development.

Conclusion

This chapter has brought together some basic evidence on the impact of protectionism on world trade in the 1930s, as well as on the patterns of protectionism across countries. The spread of trade barriers inflicted substantial damage on world trade, accounting for about half the reduction in trade in the early

1930s. In addition, the pattern of protectionism across countries is consistent with the trilemma interpretation, namely, that changes in exchange rates and trade controls were substitutes for one another. Finally, trade restrictions proved to be a poor substitute for exchange rate and monetary policy changes as a means of promoting economic recovery. The implication is that if more countries had been willing to adjust their exchange rates in the early 1930s, the outbreak of destructive protection, and the prolongation of the Great Depression, could have been avoided.

4 Conclusions

Free trade and fixed exchange rates are incompatible in the modern world. . . . [A]ll modern free traders should be in favor of variable exchange rates.
—James Meade

Throughout this book we have seen that the extreme protectionism of the 1930s grew out of the conflict between fixed exchange rates and open trade policies. Countries that maintained a fixed exchange rate ran into balance-of-payments difficulties. They sought to prop up overvalued currencies and stem gold outflows by using exchange controls and import restrictions to reduce spending on foreign goods. Other countries escaped their balance-of-payments difficulties by allowing their currencies to depreciate. They no longer had to worry about maintaining a fixed exchange rate and, consequently, did not have to adopt protectionist trade policies to the same extent as those that tried to keep the exchange rate fixed.

Thus, the protectionism of the 1930s emerged as a consequence of the reluctance to use the exchange rate as an adjustment mechanism and the substitution of import controls instead.[1] As it turned out, this was a disastrous choice. Abandoning the gold standard and allowing one's currency to depreciate was good for economic recovery and good for open trade policies. Staying on the gold standard and maintaining the gold parity was bad for both; it postponed the recovery and was a breeding ground for protectionism. And leaving the gold standard did not lead to uncontrollable inflation, as many had feared. In the end, there was no real trade-off between the two policies at all.

In this concluding chapter, we take a closer look at the relationship between the exchange rate regime and trade policy. In addition, we consider the distinction between mercantilism and protectionism and, finally, explore why the worldwide recession of 2009 did not lead to a trade policy disaster similar to that of the 1930s.

Exchange Rate Regimes and Trade Policy

Although economists today usually treat international trade and international finance as separate fields of study, the events of the 1930s suggest that the two are intimately linked. As Bidwell (1932, 400) noted, "if this depression has proved anything it is that international trade and international finance are fundamentally inseparable." In particular, the exchange rate regime played a significant role in shaping the trade policies that grew out of the Great Depression.

With fixed exchange rates, a country's central bank is required to intervene in the foreign exchange market to

---

1. What Max Corden (1997, 276) has written about in a different context has applicability here: "the inability to use the exchange rate as a policy instrument provides an incentive to impose or increase restrictive trade policies at times of crisis, and thus leads to protectionist measures which often fail to be reduced when the short-term crisis is at an end."

maintain a specified price of domestic currency in terms of gold or other currencies. As we have seen, this requirement imposed a major constraint on policymakers in the early 1930s and pushed trade policy in a protectionist direction. The link between fixed exchange rates and protectionist trade policies is rooted in the balance of payments. Under fixed exchange rates, a country's policymakers have to pay close attention to the level of reserves held by the central bank. The balance of trade was an important determinant of net gold flows between countries, and hence of changes in those reserves. Changes in reserves affected a country's monetary policy, which in turn affected the economy's performance.

Therefore, under fixed exchange rates, government policies to reduce imports could potentially improve the balance of trade and increase a country's reserves, which could allow an easing of monetary conditions and stimulate the domestic economy when factors of production are not fully employed. In contrast, there is no clear link between flexible exchange rates and protectionist trade policies because in this case monetary policy is not tied to the trade balance and the level of the central bank's reserves.

How did this relationship play out in during the Great Depression? At the start, most countries had fixed exchange rates under the gold standard. In the late 1920s, the United States and France began to accumulate gold. The result, a loss of reserves in other countries, triggered tighter monetary policies and put the world economy under enormous deflationary pressure. There were three ways of adjusting to this situation, none of them desirable: the continued deflation of wages and prices, changes to the exchange rate (gold parity), or the imposition of trade controls to reduce imports. Most countries tried deflation for several years, but it only seemed to intensify the economic slump. Most countries resisted changing the gold parity because it was feared that the depreciation of one's currency would lead to monetary instability and uncontrolled inflation. This left only trade restrictions, which could be used to reduce spending on foreign goods and thereby stem the outflow of gold reserves.[2]

The decision to restrict imports proved disastrous in the highly deflationary environment of the early 1930s. Not only did it contribute to the demise of the world trading system, it was a wholly inadequate substitute for a more expansionary monetary policy. By postponing the decision to allow the exchange rate to change and use monetary policy to address the crisis, trade policy interventions prolonged the Great Depression. Thus, the decisions made about exchange rate policy in the face of declining reserves were fateful. Instead of allowing the exchange rate to adjust, many governments imposed trade controls on the grounds that it was the least objectionable course of action. In retrospect, this was a grave mistake.[3]

2. In its review of interwar economic policy, the League of Nations (1942a, 146) pointed to the fear of inflation as a key reason why countries avoided devaluation and resisted efforts at trade liberalization: "there were two other factors of steadily increasing importance working against the acceptance of the recommendations made in favour of more liberal trade policies during the depression: (a) the obstructions imposed by what were in fact the semi-concealed military policies of certain states; and (b) the inhibitions caused by recent experience which rendered many of the recommendations unacceptable. Of these inhibitions, by far the most important was the fear of inflation which was deeply imbedded in the minds of the public in all those countries that had passed through a period of hyper-inflation in the 20's. This fear, coupled with a widespread misunderstanding of the nature and causes of inflation, led the governments of many of those countries to reject immutably all proposals in favour of devaluation."

3. Given the chronic deflation of the early 1930s, it is ironic that opposition to monetary inflation was so widely and strongly held. Yet the disastrous experience of inflation in the early 1920s led many people to equate going off the gold standard with precisely such an outcome.

In the 1940s, when economists and policymakers were trying to draw lessons from the 1930s for the creation of a new postwar economic system, the interaction between the exchange rate regime and trade policy was imperfectly understood. The most commonly drawn trade policy lesson was that protectionism could be avoided through domestic policies that prevented recessions and ensured full employment. At the end of his *General Theory*, John Maynard Keynes (1936, 382) expressed this hope:

> if nations can learn to provide themselves with full employment by their domestic policy . . . there need be no important economic forces calculated to set the interest of one country against that of its neighbors. . . . International trade would cease to be what it is, namely, a desperate expedient to maintain employment at home by forcing sales on foreign markets and restricting purchases, which, if successful, will merely shift the problem of unemployment to the neighbor which is worsted in the struggle, but a willing and unimpeded exchange of goods and services in conditions of mutual advantage.[4]

But what if domestic policies to ensure full employment conflicted with balance-of-payments equilibrium? In particular, what if concerns about the balance of payments prevented monetary and fiscal policies from being used to achieve full employment? This question led James Meade to distinguish between internal balance (full-employment equilibrium) and external balance (balance-of-payments equilibrium). He and others investigated the appropriate policies to achieve both internal and external balance while also permitting open

---

4. In his review of the 1930s, Heinz Arndt (1944, 275) wrote that unless countries "learn to maintain full employment at home by other methods, the temptation to shift the burden on to other countries by striving for the most favorable possible balances of trade is bound to prove irresistible."

trade policies.[5] In his view, flexible exchange rates would ensure external balance and leave monetary policy free to help ensure internal balance.

Yet most economists and policymakers preferred to have fixed exchange rates after World War II, despite the constraints that fixed rates put on monetary policy. Somewhat paradoxically, the desire for stable exchange rates and the fear of floating exchange rates were seen at the time as having been reinforced by the events of the 1930s. Ragnar Nurkse, in an otherwise impressive analysis, *The Interwar Currency Experience*, published in 1944 by the League of Nations, reflected this view. "If there is anything that inter-war experience has clearly demonstrated," Nurkse (1944, 137–138) wrote, "it is that paper currency exchanges cannot be left free to fluctuate from day to day under the influence of market supply and demand." Nurkse believed that "if currencies are left free to fluctuate, 'speculation' in the widest sense is likely to play havoc with exchange rates." This would create risks that would discourage international trade and jeopardize domestic economic stability.

Although this was arguably a misreading of the 1930s experience, Nurkse's conclusion reflected the consensus view at the time. Even Keynes, who had been an opponent of the gold standard, favored exchange rate stability and was skeptical that flexible exchange rates could solve balance-of-payments

---

5. This work led to what David Vines (2003) has called the "creation of international macroeconomics." As Jagdish Bhagwati (1988, 129) noted in his 1987 Ohlin Lectures: "Good microeconomics presupposes good macroeconomics. It was not for nothing that Nobel laureate James Meade's classic work on the theory of international economic policy had two volumes, one on balance-of-payments management and a second (in proper sequence) on the theory of commercial policy. The experiences of the interwar period and the 1970s underline the importance of proper macroeconomic management if we are to be able politically to manage trade policies so as to reap the gains from trade."

problems.[6] This led him, in the early 1940s, to be quite illiberal in his approach to trade policy, particularly in his insistence that quantitative import restrictions would be needed to address payments imbalances after the war.

Not all economists agreed with this preference for fixed exchange rates and import controls. Keynes's friends, James Meade and Marcus Fleming, argued with him quite vigorously over the merits of exchange rate adjustments versus import controls as a means of achieving balance-of-payments equilibrium.[7] Meade in particular was one of the few economists of the period who consistently argued that free and open trade was a more important policy objective than fixed exchange rates, and therefore exchange rates should be determined by the market. He strongly believed that, by depriving a country of an independent monetary policy, fixed exchange rates would take away a potentially powerful tool for achieving internal balance. In addition to interfering with a country's ability to address an economic slump, fixed exchange rates would open the door for trade controls. Not only would

---

6. As he put it, "I have no sympathy with the idea, which . . . I regard as vestigial, that, if imports have to be restricted, it is in some way sounder to raise their prices by deprecation of the exchanges than by any other technique" (Keynes 1971–1988, 26:289). In 1943, Hubert Henderson (1955, 292) similarly concluded, "the interwar experience suggests that exchange-rate alternations cannot serve as the mainspring of a self-adjusting system" and "it may become necessary for the individual country to regulate its balance of payments by deliberate action." Donald Moggridge (1986, 66–67) remarks, "By the time Keynes came to draft his proposals for the post–World War II monetary system, he had at one time or another recommended almost every exchange rate regime known to modern analysts except completely floating exchange rates."

7. See Keynes (1971–1988, 26:289ff). Bertil Ohlin (1945, 37) seemed to be sympathetic to Meade and Fleming's position and offered a cautious assessment: "in certain circumstances, it may be far better that a State should make some minor adjustment to the foreign exchange rate of its currency than it should be tempted to take measures" that would restrict imports.

such controls reduce trade and economic efficiency, they were generally ill-suited to promoting the underlying goal of a balance-of-payments adjustment.

In 1944, when policymakers from around the world gathered at the Bretton Woods Conference to establish the postwar international monetary system, they opted for a "fixed but adjustable" exchange rate regime. The final agreement acknowledged that countries might need to change the value of their currency in the face of balance-of-payments disequilibrium, and thus exchange rates were adjustable in principle. However, such changes were discouraged, and countries were very reluctant to change their parity in practice.

Thus, the architects of the postwar system chose to constrain a country's monetary and exchange rate policy just as it had been in the 1930s, albeit this time to the U.S. dollar, which fortunately was growing more rapidly in supply than gold had been. But because the constraint on monetary policy still existed, Meade always regretted the decision to adopt fixed exchange rates. Decades later, he still expressed dismay at the "fundamentally ill-judged system of the adjustable peg" in the Bretton Woods agreement.[8] Meade thought that fixed exchange rates had no place in the set of policies that would make free trade, full employment, and a balance-of-payments equilibrium compatible with one another. In a classic essay, "The Case for Variable Exchange Rates," Meade (1955, 6) stated: "free trade and fixed exchange rates are incompatible in the modern world; and all

8. In his 1977 Nobel lecture, Meade (1978, 434) stated: "In my opinion there was one important original flaw in this system, namely the insistence on the International Monetary Fund's very sticky adjustable peg mechanism for the correction of inappropriate exchange rates. . . . Variations in the rate of exchange between the national currencies combined with freedom of trade and payments should in my view be the normal instrument of such foreign exchange policies."

modern free traders should be in favor of variable exchange rates."[9]

Why did the architects of the postwar system adopt a fixed exchange rate regime without seriously considering an alternative? At least three factors explain the decision: the fear of inflation, the fear of disrupting world trade, and the fear of "competitive devaluations."

As we have seen, despite the severe deflation of the early 1930s, memories of the high inflation of the early 1920s still inspired fear. As a result, policymakers believed that stable exchange rates were needed to maintain stable domestic prices. Unfortunately, this confused cause and effect: it was the instability in prices that led to the instability in exchange rates, not the other way around.

A second reason for the decision to adopt fixed exchange rates was the expectation that market-determined exchange rates would gyrate wildly and discourage world trade. The few proponents of flexible rates conceded that exchange rates would fluctuate, but they believed that the impact on world trade would be minimal because forward markets could be used to hedge exchange rate risk. They acknowledged that stable exchange rates encouraged trade, but argued that fixed exchange rates constrained domestic policy and gave

9. Milton Friedman (1953b, 217) was similarly critical of the postwar policy constraints: "The postwar system of exchange rates, temporarily rigid but subject to change from time to time by government action, can provide neither the certainty about exchange rates and the freedom from irresponsible governmental action of a fully operative gold standard, nor the independence of each country from the monetary vagaries of other countries, nor the freedom of each country to pursue internal monetary stability in its own way that are provided by truly flexible exchange rates. This postwar system sacrifices the simultaneous achievement of the two major objectives of vigorous multilateral trade and independence of internal monetary policy on the altar of the essentially minor objective of a rigid exchange rate."

the system as a whole a protectionist bias. By discouraging exchange rate changes, countries would have to use import restrictions to achieve external balance, something that could pose an even more significant obstacle to world trade than fluctuating exchange rates.

Finally, a fixed exchange rate regime seemed desirable to those who saw exchange rate changes in the 1930s as "competitive devaluations," as a beggar-my-neighbor policy that improved the competitive position of one country at the expense of others. To prevent this problem in the postwar era, the Articles of Agreement of the International Monetary Fund required that countries "avoid manipulating exchange rates or the international monetary system in order to prevent effective balance of payments adjustment or to gain an unfair competitive advantage over other members" (Article IV:1(iii)).[10]

Unfortunately, concerns about competitive devaluation were also based on a misreading of the historical experience. In fact, countries did not "devalue" their currencies in the 1930s to give their exports a competitive advantage over their rivals. As we saw in chapter 2, most countries were forced to devalue (or allow their currencies to depreciate) because they were facing a massive loss of gold reserves. Countries fought valiantly against the foreign exchange market pressure on their currencies by raising interest rates and borrowing emergency reserves from other central banks. For example, the Bank of England resisted the selling pressure on the pound for many weeks, but eventually decided that it was a losing battle and efforts to keep the pound at the gold parity were no longer worth the loss of additional gold and foreign exchange reserves. As Hubert Henderson (1955, 259) recalled:

10. Articles of Agreement can be found at http://www.imf.org/external/pubs/ft/aa/index.htm.

The idea that the British departure from the gold standard was influenced by a desire to devalue the pound is entirely baseless. We were driven off gold, despite strenuous efforts to remain on. Nonetheless, we soon found that the fall of the exchange brought substantial compensations with it; and the sense that the overvalued pound of the later 1920s had been an incubus of which we were well rid became general.

For all practical purposes, the notion that countries engaged in competitive devaluation during the 1930s is simply erroneous. In fact, there was only one real example of a competitive devaluation. After New Zealand devalued its currency by 15 percent against the British pound in 1933, Denmark followed with a 17 percent devaluation of the krona. New Zealand's primary motivation was not to improve export performance but to redistribute income to the depressed farm sector. Denmark followed because, like New Zealand, it was also a major exporter of butter to the British market and did not want its exports to suffer.[11] Furthermore, as we saw in chapter 3, "competitive devaluation" was not necessarily a beggar-my-neighbor policy because it had expansionary effects that positively affected other trading partners.

The concerns about inflation, world trade, and competitive devaluations led officials at the Bretton Woods Conference to establish a system of fixed but adjustable exchange rates. But governments also wanted to do away with the protectionist measures that blocked the flow of world trade. Thus, they sought to combine fixed exchange rates with trade liberalization, even though these two policies sometimes conflicted. This created a built-in tension between the international

---

11. "The devaluation of the New Zealand pound in 1933 was intended not to improve the competitiveness of Dominion exports, but to spread the costs of the depression more evenly by raising relative farm prices," Greasley and Oxley (2002, 698) note. On this devaluation episode, see Straumann (2010, 121) and Kindleberger (1934).

monetary system, represented by the International Monetary Fund, and the international trading system, represented by the General Agreement on Tariffs and Trade. This tension is reflected in Article XII of the GATT, which permits the use of trade measures for balance-of-payments purposes.[12]

As it turned out, because countries were reluctant to change the value of their currencies during the 1950s and 1960s, they often turned to import restrictions instead. Between 1955 and 1971, nine industrial countries used import surcharges to address balance-of-payments problems in the hopes of avoiding any exchange rate changes.[13] For example, from June 1962 to April 1963, Canada imposed import restrictions to support the Canadian dollar. In October 1964, Britain imposed a 15 percent import surcharge to defend the fixed exchange rate. This was reduced to 10 percent in February 1965 and finally eliminated in November 1966. With the dollar as the anchor currency, the United States could not devalue itself when it ran into balance-of-payments deficits in the late 1960s. But in August 1971 it imposed a 10 percent import surcharge to force other countries to revalue their currencies against the dollar. When other countries did so in December 1971, the surcharge was dropped.

---

12. According to Article XII of the GATT, "any contracting party, in order to safeguard its external financial position and its balance of payments, may restrict the quantity or value of merchandise permitted to be imported, subject to the provisions of the following paragraphs of this Article. . . . [The] import restrictions instituted, maintained or intensified by a contracting party under this Article shall not exceed those necessary: (i) to forestall the imminent threat of, or to stop, a serious decline in its monetary reserves, or (ii) in the case of a contracting party with very low monetary reserves, to achieve a reasonable rate of increase in its reserves."

13. Bergsten (1977) reports that import surcharges were used by France (1954–1958, 1968), Denmark (1955–1956, 1971–1972), Sweden (1959–1960), Spain (1958–1959, 1965–1971), Canada (1962–1963), the United Kingdom (1964–1966, 1968–1970), Germany (1968), the United States (1971), and Italy (1974–1975).

Although each of these measures was temporary, lasting from a few months to two years, the import surcharges
had significant effects on trade. The duties were much more
substantial than the most important multilateral tariff reductions negotiated during the Bretton Woods period, namely,
the Kennedy Round of GATT negotiations, which began
in 1963 and concluded in 1967. The European Economic
Community's average tariff on nonagricultural dutiable imports was 12.8 percent before the round and 8.1 percent after,
a reduction of five percentage points. The import surcharges
usually consisted of a 10 percent across-the-board tariff
on imports, much larger than the Kennedy Round cuts. Of
course, the import surcharges were temporary, whereas the
cuts were permanent, but they still provoked sharp criticism
and were a source of friction among trading partners.

The import surcharges also proved ineffective in providing
a long-term solution to the underlying balance-of-payments
problem. The surcharge delayed but did not avert an eventual devaluation. "In every instance where trade measures
were adopted by a major country, they failed to prevent a
subsequent exchange-rate change," Bergsten (1977, 3) notes.
Examples include the French devaluation in 1958, the British
devaluation in 1967, and the French devaluation and German
revaluation in 1969. Fortunately, since the policies were substitutes for one another, import surcharges were lifted once
the depreciation in the exchange rate helped to improve the
country's balance-of-payments position.

The postwar trade policy experience of developing countries under fixed exchange rates was even more problematic.
Although the goal of fixed rates was to provide monetary
discipline and curb inflation, they often did so imperfectly,
with the usual result being an overvalued currency. Developing countries then turned to import controls, such as

quantitative restrictions and exchange controls, to compensate for the overvaluation and relieve pressures on the balance of payments.[14] Such controls tended to accumulate in the period prior to devaluation, with the resulting compression of imports, but they almost always failed to prevent an eventual devaluation. Although the devaluation should have permitted the import controls to be removed, the controls, once imposed, tended to remain in place for an extended period because they sheltered special interests, which now had a stake in perpetuating them.

Misaligned exchange rates accompanied by import restrictions have been linked to poor economic performance in developing countries, including slow economic growth. As Schatz and Tarr (2002, 17) note:

Although as a group, developing countries progressively liberalized their trade regimes during the 1980s and 1990s, some governments continue to take actions to defend their exchange rates that are counter to their long-run trade liberalization efforts. One classic pattern is to attempt to defend an overvalued exchange rate through protectionist trade policies. Experience shows that protection in defense of an overvalued exchange rate will significantly retard the economy's medium-to-long term growth prospects. In fact, an overvalued exchange rate is often the root cause of protection, and the country will be unable to return to the more

---

14. Developing countries have a long history of resisting devaluation and using import restrictions to address balance-of-payments problems. Schatz and Tarr (2002) provide a recent survey of the link between exchange rate misalignment and trade protection in developing countries. Edwards (1989, 177) reports that "in the great majority of cases the devaluation was preceded by an important piling up of exchange controls and [trade] restrictions." Little and colleagues (1993, 273) find that "a country that seeks to maintain a fixed exchange rate and encounters a balance of payments problem is likely to impose or tighten import restrictions. . . . Econometric evidence confirms the hypothesis that trade policy tightening and devaluations were substitutes up to 1983."

liberal trade policies that allow growth without an exchange rate adjustment.[15]

In the 1990s, transition economies in Eastern Europe faced the same trade-offs between their exchange rate policy and their trade policy. The former Communist countries of Bulgaria, the Czech Republic, Hungary, and Poland, aimed to stabilize their nominal exchange rates, but failed to contain domestic inflation or improve their productivity performance. As a result, their currencies became overvalued. The appreciation of the real exchange rate put a squeeze on export and import-competing industries and led to protectionist pressures. Rather than adjust the nominal exchange rate, these countries resorted to import surcharges and other trade restrictions (Drabek and Brada 1998). These policies interfered with their foreign trade without solving the underlying problem of the exchange rate misalignment.

Much like the interwar gold standard, the Bretton Woods system of "fixed but adjustable" exchange rates was relatively short-lived. It lasted from 1958, when exchange controls were abolished and currency convertibility was established, until 1971, when President Richard Nixon closed the gold window. With the move to floating exchange rates in 1973, the rationale for using import restrictions for balance-of-payments purposes disappeared. In fact, one of the benefits of floating exchange rates was that countries no longer had a balance-of-payments "problem" in the sense that governments no longer needed to hold gold or foreign exchange reserves to support a given level of the exchange rate.

---

15. In a study of trade liberalization and developing countries, Michaely, Papageorgiou, and Choksi (1991, 276) report that "a nominal devaluation does appear to be almost a necessary condition . . . for the ultimate sustainability of a [trade] liberalization policy."

The shift to flexible exchange rates also undermined the macroeconomic case for trade policy interventions that had existed with fixed exchange rates. The textbook Mundell-Fleming open economy model illustrates how the efficacy of protectionist measures declined in moving from fixed to flexible exchange rates. Under fixed exchange rates, an import restriction diverts domestic expenditure from foreign goods to domestic goods. Because the exchange rate is fixed, there is no adverse effect on the country's exports, and therefore the policy can potentially expand domestic output. However, under floating exchange rates, the reduction in imports is accompanied by an appreciation of the exchange rate, which reduces exports and leaves domestic output unchanged. Furthermore, "under floating rates, tariffs and quotas, even if they seem to have favorable direct macroeconomic effects, produce unfavorable indirect effects," Krugman (1982) has noted. "Under a variety of assumptions, the indirect effects will be larger: under floating rates, protection will often turn out to be a contractionary policy."[16] Thus, floating exchange rates undermine the macroeconomic case for using trade policy measures to boost domestic output.

Flexible exchange rates may even have facilitated the liberalization of trade policy in the 1980s and 1990s. Of course, the move to flexible exchange rates has not eliminated special interest demands for trade protection. A large number of studies show that an appreciation of the exchange rate is often associated with the increasing use of import restrictions, such

16. He continues, "The verdict on protection as a macroeconomic tool, then, is negative. Tariffs and quotas seem likely to do more harm than good even from a purely nationalist point of view, with quotas looking worse. If nationalistic protection gives rise to a trade war, the conventional microeconomic losses from restricted trade will probably be dwarfed by severe macroeconomic losses as output contracts around the world" (1982, 179).

as antidumping duties. Still, where exchange rates have not been fully flexible, such as China's recent policy with respect to the renminbi, conflicts over trade have been more frequent.

In sum, although the relationship between exchange rate regimes and trade policy not been the subject of much economic research, there are clearly linkages between the two. In particular, the desire to maintain fixed exchange rates seems to have pushed trade policy in a protectionist direction not only during the 1930s but in other periods of history as well.

Protectionism or Mercantilism?

This book has followed the standard practice of economists of referring to import restrictions as "protectionist." The usual goal of such policies is to increase domestic output by reducing imports of goods that compete with those produced at home. Such measures are often blamed on lobbying by special interests, particularly the domestic industry, which stands to benefit from such trade barriers. But this way of thinking about the trade restrictions that proliferated during the 1930s is not entirely accurate. Instead, the trade restrictions of that period were more "mercantilist" in the sense of trying to improve the balance of trade and stem the outflow of gold reserves.[17] This distinction deserves some elaboration.

During the 1930s, contemporary observers frequently complained that "nationalism" and "economic interests" were forces that were pushing governments to erect barriers to international trade. While political pressures to limit imports are always present, the protectionism of the 1930s was

---

17. Mercantilism refers to the body of economic thought that emerged in early seventeenth-century England and is commonly thought to have put emphasis on the balance of trade as a way of increasing the wealth of a country.

much more pervasive than can be explained by the lobbying of special interest groups. During the Great Depression, few countries or industries were facing the surge of imports that typically elicits a protectionist response. As we have seen, import penetration, as measured by the import-to-GDP ratio, was actually declining as the world economy entered the Depression. With imports falling more rapidly than production, foreign competition was in many cases becoming less of a problem for domestic producers. Therefore, it is difficult to believe that special interests were the most important factor behind the outbreak of protectionism.[18]

What, then, led policymakers to impose import restrictions? As we have seen, the answer lies in powerful macroeconomic forces and the constraints on the response of policymakers. Struggling to cope with balance-of-payments difficulties, many countries turned to trade restrictions as a potential remedy. Hence, the primary motivation for the trade policies of the 1930s was not so much protecting domestic industries from foreign competition as protecting gold reserves from being drained away. The goal was to reduce

---

18. "While the extent to which the pressure of sectional groups was responsible for the growth and maintenance of barriers to international trade has sometimes been exaggerated, it certainly played a significant part in the commercial policies of most countries," Arndt (1944, 277–278) conceded. "But, quite apart from the fact that such cases were probably insignificant by comparison with the magnitude of the international economic problem as whole, the question may again be asked how insistent the pressure of sectional interests would have been in expanding rather than stagnating economies." Arndt argued that the real underlying problem was not special interests but the failure of government policy to provide economic stability and full employment: "but for the failure to solve what were essentially technical economic problems . . . both economic nationalism and 'vested interests' might have been relatively innocuous. To put the blame for the growth of trade barriers, or for any of the other economic evils of the interwar period, on the prevalence of economic nationalism and the pressure of vested interests is to blind our eyes to these economic problems."

total spending on foreign goods, even if the imports did not compete with domestic producers, so that foreign exchange would be conserved and the balance of trade improved. For example, the purpose of French import quotas was not simply to increase the domestic production of goods that substituted for imports but to limit spending on foreign goods in order to compensate for an overvalued exchange rate, improve the balance of trade, and safeguard gold reserves. Certainly Germany's policy of near autarky was driven by the need to conserve foreign exchange and created enormous disruptions for its industries at the time. Because imports often supplied raw materials necessary for domestic production, the policy of reducing imports was not always intended to stimulate domestic output but to strengthen the balance of payments.

Of course, protectionism is not incompatible with mercantilism, and there is no inherent conflict between the two. The goals and underlying motivation, however, are different. Protectionism is selective and favors certain industries with government assistance. Mercantilism implies much more pervasive restrictions on trade in order to reduce overall spending on imports.[19]

Ever since the days of David Hume and Adam Smith, economists have been highly critical of mercantilist doctrine for its preoccupation with the balance of trade. Hume proposed the price-specie flow mechanism to show that mercantilist concerns about the balance of trade were misplaced because domestic prices would adjust automatically to

---

19. Jacob Viner (1937, 73) also made the distinction between mercantilism and protectionism and noted that they differed more in emphasis than in actual content. He observed that modern protectionists want to restrict "imports of foreign goods of a kind which can be produced at home in order that domestic production and employment may be fostered," but did not "lay special stress on the desirability of increasing or maintain the national stock of bullion."

restore equilibrium. Smith attacked mercantilists for supposedly confusing precious metals with national wealth and for thinking that international trade is a zero-sum game in which one country wins and another country loses.

But these criticisms lose some force when one thinks about how the economy functioned under the interwar gold standard. The price-specie flow mechanism that brings about changes in domestic prices did not operate smoothly and without friction. Any country experiencing a loss of gold was likely to experience deflation, which could put the economy into a severe downturn. As Gustav Cassel (1933, 21) argued, "The notion that the fall in prices is a natural process to which we must submit has been proclaimed during the whole period in which the deflation has been proceeding, those who proclaim it having learnt nothing from the terrible consequences which the deflation has entailed."[20] In fact, even Hume recognized that deflation brought with it significant problems. He argued that the absolute quantity of money in a country was less important than that it be kept increasing rather than decreasing. A falling money supply, in his words, would keep a country "weaker and more miserable" than other countries where the stock of money was increasing.[21]

---

20. According to Cassel (1933, 21), those who argued for continued deflation during the Great Depression "entirely ignore the difficulties of such 'adjustment,' and insist on enforcing it at any cost. They do not see that the pressure which has to be exerted for this purpose will lead to a further depression of commodity prices, so that in this way equilibrium can never be restored. They do not trouble about the social strife which a forced reduction of wages is bound to provoke, and they demand that even existing debts shall be adjusted to the falling price-level, without realizing what a complete economic ruin is bound to follow on such spread of insolvency."

21. As Hume ([1752] 1955, 39–40) put it: "The good policy of the magistrate consists only in keeping it, if possible, still encreasing; because, by that means, he keeps alive a spirit of industry in the nation, and encreases the stock of labour, in which consists all real power and riches. A nation, whose

If a country losing gold wanted to avoid the painful process of deflation but was unwilling to adjust the exchange rate, then government policies to reduce imports and improve the balance of trade could slow the loss of gold reserves. Furthermore, there actually is a zero-sum aspect to the monetary system under a gold standard. Because the international supply of gold is fixed in the short run, a country can increase its domestic gold reserves, and hence its money supply, only by taking gold from others. When the world's gold reserves are fixed and countries want to hold more reserves, one country's gain is another country's loss.

In the final chapter of his *General Theory*, Keynes included a short but provocative section entitled "Notes on Mercantilism," in which he argued that there was an "element of scientific truth in mercantilist doctrine." According to Keynes, mercantilist writers held that the rate of interest was governed by the quantity of precious metals in a country. Since a favorable balance of trade was the only method of increasing the quantity of precious metals in a country that did not produce them, a favorable balance of trade was a way of keeping the domestic interest rate low. In his view, therefore, mercantilists were justified in their concerns over the balance of trade.

However, in the *General Theory*, although not later as a government adviser, Keynes (1936, 338) rejected import restrictions as a way of improving the balance of trade:

money decreases, is actually, at that time, weaker and more miserable than another nation, which possesses no more money, but is on the encreasing hand. This will be easily accounted for, if we consider, that the alterations in the quantity of money, either on one side or the other, are not immediately attended with proportionable alterations in the price of commodities. There is always an interval before matters be adjusted to their new situation; and this interval is as pernicious to industry, when gold and silver are diminishing, as it is advantageous when these metals are encreasing."

It does not follow from this that the maximum degree of restriction of import will promote the maximum favourable balance of trade . . . an immoderate policy may lead to a senseless international competition for a favourable balance which injures all alike . . . [and] a policy of trade restrictions is a treacherous instrument even for the attainment of its ostensible object, since private interest, administrative incompetence and the intrinsic difficult of the task may divert it into producing results directly opposite to those intended.

Rather than endorsing trade restrictions, Keynes (1936, 339) argued that "the weight of my criticism is directed against the inadequacy of the *theoretical* foundations of the *laissez-faire* doctrine . . . against the notion that the rate of interest and the volume of investment are self-adjusting at the optimum level, so that preoccupation with the balance of trade is a waste of time." While Keynes believed that mercantilist writers perceived a problem without being able to solve it, he faulted classical writers for ignoring it altogether.[22]

Keynes's rehabilitation of mercantilism sparked a minor controversy, but his interpretation received some support from subsequent economic historians who studied conditions at the time when mercantilist writers were penning their tracts. That is, domestic monetary difficulties and a shortage of specie in early seventeenth-century England were related to the problems of maintaining a favorable balance of trade.[23]

---

22. Keynes rejected the view that adjustment to equilibrium would be automatic: "Under the influence of this faulty theory the City of London gradually devised the most dangerous technique for the maintenance of equilibrium which can be possibly imagined, namely, the technique of bank rate coupled with a rigid parity of the foreign exchanges. For this meant that the objective of maintaining a domestic rate of interest consistent with full employment was wholly ruled out. . . . Recently, practical bankers in London have learned much, and one can almost hope that in Great Britain the technique of bank rate will never be used again to protect the foreign balance in conditions in which it is likely to cause unemployment at home."

23. See, for example, Wilson (1949), Supple (1959), and Coleman (1980).

Because of the economic problems caused by deflation, mercantilist writers may have been justified in their concerns about the balance of trade and the flow of bullion across countries.

All of this has some relevance to understanding the Great Depression. If a few countries tried to accumulate gold reserves, others would be put under deflationary pressure. As we saw in chapter 1, this was precisely the situation in the late 1920s and early 1930s. The United States, which had been exporting gold in the mid-1920s, began importing it after tightening its monetary policy in 1928. And France undertook policies that enabled it to increase its share of world gold reserves from 7 percent in 1927 to 27 percent in 1932. Even worse, these countries sterilized the gold inflows, preventing the price-specie flow mechanism from working as it was supposed to.

This "gold hoarding" created an artificial shortage of reserves and gave rise to deflationary pressure in the rest of the world. Given the economic and social costs of deflation, it is understandable that other countries did not want their monetary policies to be held hostage to the attempts by some central banks to accumulate gold reserves. Unless these countries were willing to change the exchange rate, however, they were driven to adopt restrictive trade policies. The eventual result, the dissolution of the gold standard, followed only after the world trading system was ruined in an attempt to hold the flawed international monetary system together. As Arndt (1944, 293) noted, "much of the tariff and currency 'warfare' of the 1930s was directly due to the impossibility of correcting maladjustments in the balance of payments by the orthodox gold standard method."

In sum, the 1930s trade policy experience can be viewed as the consequences of countries undertaking desperate measures to limit spending on foreign goods and conserve gold reserves. The disastrous trade policies arose out of the malfunctioning international monetary system. While the import restrictions of the decade have been labeled "protectionist," the term "mercantilist" is probably a more accurate description.

Averting Protectionism in the Great Recession

The financial crisis that came with the October 2008 collapse of Lehman Brothers, and the ensuing worldwide recession, have often been compared to the stock market crash of October 1929 and the onset of the Great Depression. In both instances, world trade fell sharply. In 2009, the volume of world trade fell 12 percent, the largest decline in the post–World War II period (figure 4.1). Although this was less than the 25 percent decline in world trade during 1929–1932, it was more than the 7 percent drop during the first year of the Depression (1930).

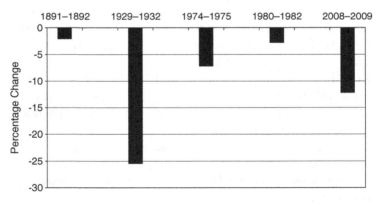

Figure 4.1
Major declines in world trade volume. *Source:* Lewis (1981), League of Nations (1939c), and World Trade Organization (2010).

Of course, world trade declined much more in the early 1930s because the underlying shock was much greater; world GDP declined about 13 percent during the three years of the Great Depression, whereas it fell less than 1 percent in 2009 and started growing again in 2010.[24] The fact that a relatively small blip in world GDP was associated with such an enormous decline in the volume of world trade has led economists to investigate the role of durable goods, the importance of intermediate goods and supply chains, and the disruption of trade financing as potential explanations.[25]

For our purposes, the most important difference between the two periods is that the 1930s were marked by rampant protectionism, something that has not been the case during the recent crisis. Chapter 3 noted that about half of the decline in world trade in the early 1930s can be attributed to higher trade barriers. Yet only 2 percent of the recent (2008–2009) decline in world trade has been blamed on higher trade barriers.[26]

Why was there so much protectionism in the 1930s and so little of it in recent years? The most important reason relates to the theme of this book: today, unlike the 1930s, most countries

24. The Depression figure comes from Angus Maddison's (2010) database and the contemporary figure from the International Monetary Fund.

25. One major difference between the 1930s and today is the change in the composition of world trade. In 1929, manufactured goods composed 40 percent of world trade. This grew to 72 percent in 2007. Because trade in manufactured goods fluctuates much more in response to changes in income than trade in food and raw materials, the decline in world trade in the early 1930s was relatively muted compared to what it would have been today. If trade in manufactured goods had been as large a share of world trade in the 1930s as it is today, world trade volume would have declined 32 percent, rather than 25 percent, between 1929 and 1932 (Almunia et al. 2010, 229).

26. Kee, Neagu, and Nicita (2010) find that the value of world trade fell 24 percent in 2009, but trade policy measures accounted for only 0.4 percentage points of this decline in trade, or about 2 percent.

do not have fixed exchange rates that they are desperate to maintain. There is no gold standard or Bretton Woods system but rather the "nonsystem" of floating exchange rates. The difference in the exchange rate regime is crucial not so much because currency movements are the most important part of the international adjustment mechanism, although they can be, but because countries with floating rates have no obstacles to using monetary policy in response to a crisis. The U.S. recovery from the Great Depression was driven by expansionary monetary policy, as Romer (1992) has shown, something that has also been true of most postwar recessions (Romer and Romer 1994). If monetary policy is deployed to maintain the fixed exchange rate, then governments will be forced to use other, less effective policies to address an economic downturn, such as restrictive trade policies.

Today, governments have many more policy instruments for dealing with financial crises and recessions than they did in the 1930s. Back then, governments were unable to use monetary policy or fiscal policy to boost the economy; monetary policy was constrained by the gold standard and fiscal policy by the balanced budget orthodoxy that meant government spending should be reduced in line with declining tax receipts. Today, expansionary monetary and fiscal policy measures have been used in the United States, the European Union, China, and elsewhere to help the economy. For example, governments faced considerable pressure to cut unemployment compensation to rein in spending during the Great Depression, whereas now, spending on such "automatic stabilizers" is largely unquestioned.

The impact of the monetary policy response in stabilizing the economy is evident from the behavior of U.S. imports. Figure 4.2 compares the path of U.S. imports in 1928–1931 and 2007–2010. For about nine months after the peak value in

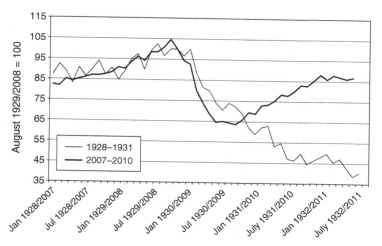

Figure 4.2
Value of U.S. merchandise imports, 1928–1931 and 2007–2010. *Source:* Business Statistics, 1932—Annual Supplement Survey of Current Business (http://fraser.stlouisfed.org/publications/business_stats/issue/133/download/1028/foreigntrade.pdf).

August 2008, U.S. imports fell at a faster pace than during the start of the Great Depression. Partly because of the aggressive action taken by the Federal Reserve, led by Ben Bernanke, a student of the Great Depression, the economy quickly stabilized and imports began growing again. In contrast, in the early 1930s, imports continued to fall because there was no significant policy response by government officials.

Although the impact of the monetary and fiscal responses to the recent worldwide recession remains controversial, they do represent policy levers that are available when governments are under pressure to do something in a crisis. As we have seen, if there is a shortage of policy instruments, government officials will reach for whatever is at their disposal.

In the case of the Great Depression, import restrictions were within easy grasp and were readily deployed.

There are other reasons why the protectionist response to the recent crisis has been relatively muted: protectionist pressures have eased considerably over time, and the ability of governments to resist such pressures has increased.

Protectionist pressures have eased, even compared to a few decades ago, for several reasons. First, foreign investment has transformed the world economy and diminished the gains to domestic producers from import restrictions. At least for the United States, so many foreign producers are now operating in its market that "domestic" firms no longer reap much benefit from trade barriers. For example, in the early 1980s, when the United States was in a deep recession, protectionist pressures were very strong. U.S. automakers demanded limits on imports of foreign cars from Japan. Today these same automakers are diversified into other markets with equity stakes in foreign producers, and foreign firms operate large production facilities in the United States. As a result, U.S.-based automakers have not asked for limits on imports because such a move would not solve any of their problems; their foreign competition is operating in the home market. Domestic industries that faced import competition in the past, including the television, automobile, steel, and semiconductor industries, have found that international diversification or joint ventures with foreign partners are a more profitable way of addressing global competition than simply stopping goods at the border.

In addition, intermediate goods now make up a greater share of world trade. The purchasers of these goods are firms, rather than households, and they want to have access to the least expensive inputs and components on the world market. International sourcing has become a routine way of doing business. The production operations and supply chains of most large firms have become so global that such firms have a vested interest in resisting protectionism rather than promoting it. Because industry associations tend to have more political clout than households, they have been a force for keeping trade open.

Another factor is that the constituency for protectionist policies is smaller than it was in the past. The share of the workforce in sectors directly affected by international trade—mainly agriculture and manufacturing—has fallen considerably. For example, in 1930, about 44 percent of the U.S. labor force was in agriculture, mining, and manufacturing. Although not all of these jobs were directly affected by imports, they were in the "tradable" sector of the economy, and some of them might have benefited from trade barriers. Today that number has dropped to 14 percent; most workers are in the service sector of the economy, which tends to be much more insulated from foreign competition. With such a small percentage of the workforce in the trade-sensitive sector of the economy, the benefits of expenditure-switching policies such as import restrictions are more limited.

The increased ability of governments to resist domestic pressures to close markets has been another important reason that protectionism has been kept at bay. Governments have been able to resist protectionist pressures because they have signed agreements and are members of institutions, such as the World Trade Organization (WTO) and the European Union (EU), that restrict the use of trade interventions. In the early 1930s, countries could impose higher trade barriers unilaterally, without violating any international agreements or necessarily anticipating much of a foreign reaction. Today, WTO rules constrain the use of discretionary trade policy interventions. Countries may be tempted to violate WTO agreements for domestic political reasons, but they will have few illusions that they will escape foreign retaliation if they do. The WTO's dispute settlement mechanism has been a deterrent to the imposition of new trade barriers, forcing countries to think twice about taking actions that will reduce imports. And the members of the EU, as a customs union, have given up their trade policy independence; they cannot raise trade barriers against one another, and EU trade policy as a whole is bound by agreements with other countries.[27]

Of course, protectionism around the world has clearly increased during the recent worldwide recession.[28] Some measures are WTO-legal, such as antidumping duties, the use of which is countercyclical and inevitably rises when economic growth falters. Many developing countries have applied tariffs that are much lower than their bound tariff commitments in the WTO. If they wanted to do so, these countries could increase their duties on imports without violating WTO rules, although this does not seem to have happened to a significant degree.

By and large, countries seem to have taken their WTO commitments seriously, and there have not been many overt attempts to break existing agreements. Unfortunately, there is also a less sanguine view. Evenett (2010) charges that "in the recent global economic downturn WTO rules did not 'hold the line' against protectionism—rather those WTO rules were

---

27. The economic policies of the individual member states of the EU are constrained on many dimensions. They have no independent trade policies, owing to the customs union, and no independent monetary policies, owing to the euro. As a result, if any particular country encounters economic difficulties, such as Spain or Greece, it does not have a monetary policy to expand or an exchange rate to depreciate, and it cannot use import controls. Hence, it must go through the painful process of domestic wage and price deflation, or what has come to be known as an "internal devaluation."

28. See the compilation by Global Trade Alert; http://www.globaltradealert.org.

circumvented and protectionist pressures were channeled into those policies where current WTO rules are weak or non-existent, or where violations are not transparent." World trade agreements are weak on such issues as subsidies and bailouts and government procurement, areas where murky protectionism has crept in. Evenett believes that "WTO rules probably affected the composition of contemporary protectionism rather than the quantum of discrimination against foreign commercial interests."

In fact, one cannot necessarily conclude from recent experience that international agreements, such as those overseen by the WTO, would necessarily constrain policymakers in an extreme situation. If the world still operated under a regime of fixed exchange rates, or if there were serious obstacles to the use of monetary and fiscal policy, such as the fear of excessive inflation or excessive public debt, the protectionist temptation might become irresistible. Despite all the WTO rules and its legal apparatus, there could be significant backsliding toward protectionism if policymakers thought that using some of these other tools of economic policy would cause more problems than breaking international trade rules.

The final but more speculative reason why protectionist pressures have been contained has to do with the idea of free trade. Keynes, of course, was famously confident about the power of economic ideas to influence policy. In this view, if economists strongly supported free trade policies, then government officials would be less inclined to adopt protectionist measures. There is mixed evidence for this idea: although the opposition of economists did nothing to prevent passage of the Smoot-Hawley Tariff Act in the United States, Keynes's willingness to endorse tariffs gave politicians the intellectual support they needed to abandon the Victorian consensus.

Still, it is true that the idea of free trade fell into disrepute during the Great Depression. Not only did the Depression discredit the doctrine of laissez-faire but the attractiveness of free trade also diminished considerably.[29] The League of Nations (1942a, 130) suggested that one reason for the failure of international conferences to stop the protectionist tide was that "the idea of freer trade was not effectively linked to that of increased welfare in the public mind, nor the idea of greater economic isolation with that of diminished welfare and increased dangers of international friction."[30]

By contrast, in the most recent crisis, the notion that free trade is a desirable economic policy was hardly challenged at all. Both economists and policymakers, as well as the business community and other groups, recognized that the financial crisis and its macroeconomic fallout had nothing to do with world trade in goods and services. Because trade was not the cause of the problems, no one has looked to trade restrictions as a potential cure. In November 2008, at the height of the financial crisis, the leaders of the G-20 issued a declaration that stated:

---

29. Reflecting the views of many in the 1930s and 1940s, Joan Robinson remarked that "as soon as the assumption of full employment is removed, the classical model for the analysis of international trade is reduced to wreckage. . . . for better or worse, international trade must be directed by conscious policy." Quoted in Irwin (1996, 201). In 1953, J. R. Hicks (1959, 41–42) noted that "free trade is no longer accepted by economists, even as an ideal, in the way that it used to be." Hicks stated that "if we are unwilling to [go right over to a system of flexible exchange rates] . . . we have got to admit that there is a strong case for import restriction, as a means of facilitating expansion without weakening the balance of payments. . . . It is this, more than anything else, which has undermined the intellectual foundations of free trade."

30. It is a tribute to the farsightedness of Scandinavian and Geneva-based economists that they kept alive the idea of freer trade between nations in policy circles (Endres and Fleming 2002). See also Ohlin (1927), Ohlin (1929), and Ohlin (1945).

We underscore the critical importance of rejecting protectionism and not turning inward in times of financial uncertainty. In this regard, within the next 12 months, we will refrain from raising new barriers to investment or to trade in goods and services, imposing new export restrictions, or implementing World Trade Organization (WTO)-inconsistent measures to stimulate exports.[31]

Even if the pledge was mainly hortatory, it at least recognized that protectionism should be resisted. Few government officials would have considered making such a pledge during the Great Depression.

To conclude, there are many reasons to hope that the trade policy experience of the 1930s will not be repeated.

Closing Remarks

The Great Depression was a terrible chapter in the history of the world economy. Fortunately, some lessons were learned from this experience. After World War II, with U.S. leadership, efforts were made under the GATT and other multilateral institutions to reduce barriers to international trade. Since then, expanding world trade—encouraged by the liberalization of trade policies in developed and developing countries alike—has been a major force promoting the growing prosperity of the world.

A significant reversal of this accomplishment would constitute another trade policy disaster. Fortunately, with flexible exchange rates having become an accepted part of the international monetary system, and with governments having more policy instruments at their disposal than they did

---

31. http://www.g20.org/Documents/g20_summit_declaration.pdf.

in the 1930s, the incentive to resort to trade restrictions has diminished. And yet severe recessions are usually a dangerous period for trade policy. Economists should always be prepared to warn against trade interventions that give the illusion of improving short-run economic prospects but that risk adverse consequences in the long run.

References

Aguado, Iago G. 2001. The Creditanstalt Crisis of 1931 and the Failure of the Austro-German Customs Union Project. *Historical Journal* 44: 199–221.

Almunia, Miguel, Agustín Bénétrix, Barry Eichengreen, Kevin H. O'Rourke, and Gisela Rua. 2010. Lessons from the Great Depression. *Economic Policy* 25:219–265.

Aparicio, Geme, Vicente Pinilla, and Raúl Serrano. 2006. Europe and the International Agricultural and Food Trade. Paper presented at the XIV International Economic History Congress, Helsinki, Finland.

Arndt, H. W. 1944. *The Economic Lessons of the 1930s.* London: Oxford University Press for the Royal Institute of International Affairs.

Bailey, Michael, Judith Goldstein, and Barry R. Weingast. 1997. The Institutional Roots of American Trade Policy: Rules, Coalitions and International Trade. *World Politics* 49:309–339.

Berg, Claes, and Lars Jonung. 1999. Pioneering Price Level Targeting: The Swedish Experience, 1931–1937. *Journal of Monetary Economics* 43:525–551.

Bergsten, C. Fred. 1977. Reforming the GATT: The Use of Trade Measures for Balance-of-Payments Purposes. *Journal of International Economics* 7:1–18.

Bernanke, Ben S. 1995. The Macroeconomics of the Great Depression: A Comparative Approach. *Journal of Money, Credit and Banking* 27 (1): 1–28.

Beveridge, William, et. al. 1931. *Tariffs: The Case Examined.* London: Longman, Greens.

Bhagwati, Jagdish. 1978. *Anatomy and Consequences of Exchange Control Regimes*. Cambridge: Ballinger.

Bhagwati, Jagdish. 1988. *Protectionism*. Cambridge, MA: MIT Press.

Bhagwati, Jagdish. 2008. *Termites in the Trading System: How Preferential Agreements Undermine Free Trade*. New York: Oxford University Press.

Bidwell, Percy W. 1932. Trade, Tariffs, the Depression. *Foreign Affairs* 10:391–401.

Bjørtvedt, Erlend, and Christian Venneslan. 1999. The Gold Standard, Trade and Recovery in the 1930s: The Norwegian Case. *Scandinavian Economic History Review* 47:23–44.

Borchardt, Knut. 1984. Could and Should Germany Have Followed Great Britain in Leaving the Gold Standard? *Journal of European Economic History* 13:471–497.

Bordo, Michael, Thomas Helbling, and Harold James. 2007. Swiss Exchange Rate Policy in the 1930s: Was the Delay in Devaluation Too High a Price to Pay for Conservatism? *Open Economies Review* 18:1–25.

Boyce, Robert W. D. 1987. *British Capitalism at the Crossroads, 1919–1932*. New York: Cambridge University Press.

Campa, Jose M. 1990. Exchange Rates and Economic Recovery in the 1930s: An Extension to Latin America. *Journal of Economic History* 50:677–682.

Carlson, Benny, and Lars Jonung. 2002. Ohlin on the Great Depression: The Popular Message in the Daily Press. In *Bertil Ohlin: A Centennial Celebration*, ed. Ronald Findlay, Lars Jonung, and Mats Lundahl. Cambridge, MA: MIT Press.

Cassel, Gustav. 1928. *Post-War Monetary Reconstruction*. New York: Columbia University Press.

Cassel, Gustav. 1933. Monetary Reconstruction. Skaddinaviska Kreditakteiebolaget, *Quarterly Report*, No. 2. April, 21–24.

Cassel, Gustav. 1934. The Restoration of the Gold Standard. Skaddinaviska Kreditakteiebolaget, *Quarterly Report*, No. 3. July.

Chipman, John S. 2007. Protection and Exchange Rates in a Small Open Economy. *Review of Development Economics* 11:205–216.

Choudhri, Ehsan, and Levis Kochin. 1980. The Exchange Rate and the International Transmission of Business Cycle Disturbances: Some Evidence from the Great Depression. *Journal of Money, Credit and Banking* 12:565–574.

Clarke, Peter. 1988. *The Keynesian Revolution in the Making.* Oxford: Clarendon Press.

Clavin, Patricia, and Jens-Wilhelm Wessels. 2004. Another Golden Idol? The League of Nations' Gold Delegation and the Great Depression, 1929–32. *International History Review* 26:765–795.

Clemens, Michael A., and Jeffrey G. Williamson. 2004. Why Did the Tariff-Growth Correlation Change after 1950? *Journal of Economic Growth* 9:5–46.

Coleman, D. C. 1980. Mercantilism Revisited. *Historical Journal* 23:773–791.

Committee on Finance and Industry. 1931. *Report.* Cmd. 3897. London: HMSO.

Corden, W. Max. 1997. *Trade Policy and Economic Welfare.* 2nd ed. New York: Oxford University Press.

Dimand, Robert. 2003. Irving Fisher on the International Transmission of Booms and Depressions through Monetary Standards. *Journal of Money, Credit and Banking* 35:49–90.

Drabek, Zdenek, and Josef C. Brada. 1998. Exchange Rate Regimes and the Stability of Trade Policy in Transitions Economies. *Journal of Comparative Economics* 26:642–668.

Dür, Andreas. 2010. *Protection for Exporters: Power and Discrimination in Transatlantic Trade Relations, 1930–2010.* Ithaca: Cornell University Press.

Edwards, Sebastian. 1989. *Real Exchange Rates, Devaluation, and Adjustment.* Cambridge, MA: MIT Press.

Eichengreen, Barry. 1981. Sterling and the Tariff, 1929–32. *Princeton Studies in International Finance* 48 (September).

Eichengreen, Barry. 1984. Keynes and Protection. *Journal of Economic History* 44:363–373.

Eichengreen, Barry. 1992. *Golden Fetters: The Gold Standard and the Great Depression.* New York: Oxford University Press.

Eichengreen, Barry, and Douglas A. Irwin. 1995. Trade Blocs, Currency Blocs, and the Reorientation of World Trade in the 1930s. *Journal of International Economics* 38:1–24.

Eichengreen, Barry, and Douglas A. Irwin. 2010. The Slide to Protectionism in the Great Depression: Who Succumbed and Why? *Journal of Economic History* 70:873–898.

Eichengreen, Barry, and Olivier Jeanne. 2000. Currency Crises and Unemployment: Britain in 1931. In *Currency Crises*, ed. Paul Krugman. Chicago: University of Chicago Press.

Eichengreen, Barry, and Jeffrey Sachs. 1985. Exchange Rates and Economic Recovery in the 1930s. *Journal of Economic History* 45:925–946.

Eichengreen, Barry, and Jeffrey Sachs. 1986. Competitive Devaluation and the Great Depression: A Theoretical Reassessment. *Economics Letters* 22:67–71.

Eichengreen, Barry, and Peter Temin. 2000. The Gold Standard and the Great Depression. *Contemporary European History* 9:183–207.

Eichengreen, Barry, and Peter Temin. 2010. Fetters of Gold and Paper. *Oxford Review of Economic Policy* 26:370–384.

Ellis, Howard S. 1941. *Exchange Control in Central Europe.* Cambridge: Harvard University Press.

Endres, Anthony M., and Grant A. Fleming. 2002. Trade Policy Research in International Organizations: The View from Geneva in the 1930s. *Journal of European Economic History* 31:645–674.

Estevadeordal, Antoni, Brian Frantz, and Alan M. Taylor. 2003. The Rise and Fall of World Trade, 1870–1939. *Quarterly Journal of Economics* 118:359–407.

Evenett, Simon. 2010. The Role of the WTO during Systemic Economic Crises. Working Paper, University of St. Gallen.

Feenstra, Robert C. 1985. Anticipated Devaluations, Currency Flight, and Direct Trade Controls in a Monetary Economy. *American Economic Review* 75:386–401.

Feinstein, Charles H., Peter Temin, and Gianni Toniolo. 2008. *The World Economy between the Wars.* New York: Oxford University Press.

Ferguson, Thomas, and Peter Temin. 2003. Made in Germany: The German Currency Crisis of 1931. *Research in Economic History* 21:1–53.

Feyrer, James. 2009. Trade and Income: Exploiting Time Series Geography. NBER Working Paper No. 14910. Cambridge, MA: National Bureau of Economic Research.

Foreman-Peck, James, Andrew Hughes-Hallett, and Yue Ma. 2007. Trade Wars and the Slump. *European Review of Economic History* 11:73–98.

Frankel, Jeffrey A., and David Romer. 1999. Does Trade Cause Growth? *American Economic Review* 89:379–399.

Frieden, Jeffry. 1997. Monetary Populism in Nineteenth-Century America: An Open Economy Interpretation. *Journal of Economic History* 57:367–395.

Friedman, Milton. 1953a. The Case for Flexible Exchange Rates. In Milton Friedman, *Essays in Positive Economics*. Chicago: University of Chicago Press.

Friedman, Milton. 1953b. Why the Dollar Shortage? *The Freeman* 4, 211–217. Reprinted in Milton Friedman, *Dollars and Deficits: Inflation, Monetary Policy and the Balance of Payments*. Englewood Cliffs, NJ: Prentice Hall, 1968.

Garside, W. R. 1998. Party Politics, Political Economy and British Protectionism, 1919-1932. *History* 83:47–65.

Gordon, Margaret. 1941. *Barriers to World Trade*. New York: Macmillan.

Gowa, Joanna, and Raymond Hicks. 2010. Did the Interwar Trade Blocs Matter? New Data and Conventional Wisdom. Unpublished working paper, Princeton University, Department of Politics.

Graham, Frank. 1949. Exchange Rates: Bound or Free? *Journal of Finance* 4:13–27.

Greasley, David, and Les Oxley. 2002. Regime Shift and Fast Recovery on the Periphery: New Zealand in the 1930s. *Economic History Review* 55:697–720.

Grossman, Richard S. 1994. The Shoe That Didn't Drop: Explaining Banking Stability During the Great Depression. *Journal of Economic History* 54:654–682.

Grytten, Ola Honningdal. 2008. Why Was the Great Depression Not So Great in the Nordic Countries? *Journal of European Economic History* 37:369–403.

Haggard, Stephan. 1988. The Institutional Foundations of Hegemony: Explaining the Reciprocal Trade Agreements Act of 1934. *International Organization* 42:91–119.

Haight, Frank A. 1935. *French Import Quotas: A New Instrument of Commercial Policy*. London: P. S. King.

Haight, Frank A. 1941. *A History of French Commercial Policies*. New York: Macmillan.

Hallwood, Paul, Ronald MacDonald, and Ian W. Marsh. 2000. An Assessment of the Causes of the Abandonment of the Gold Standard by the U.S. in 1933. *Southern Economic Journal* 67:448–459.

Hamilton, James. 1987. Monetary Factors in the Great Depression. *Journal of Monetary Economics* 19:145–169.

Hamilton, James D. 1988. Role of the International Gold Standard in Propagating the Great Depression. *Contemporary Policy Issues* 6:67–89.

Hart, Michael. 2002. *A Trading Nation: Canadian Trade Policy from Colonialism to Globalization*. Vancouver: University of British Columbia Press.

Hedberg, Peter, and Elias Håkansson. 2008. Did Germany Exploit Its Small Trading Partners? The Nature of German Interwar and Wartime Trade Policies Revisited from the Swedish Experience. *Scandinavian Economic History Review* 56:246–270.

Henderson, Hubert D. 1955. *The Interwar Years and Other Papers*. Oxford: Clarendon Press.

Hicks, J. R. 1959. Free Trade and Modern Economics [1953]. In *Essays in World Economics*. Oxford: Clarendon Press.

Hiscox, Michael. 1999. The Magic Bullet? The RTAA, Institutional Reform, and Trade Liberalization. *International Organization* 53:669–698.

Hume, David. (1752) 1955. Of Money. In *Writings on Economics*, ed. Eugene Rotwein. Madison: University of Wisconsin Press.

Hynes, William, David S. Jacks, and Kevin H. O'Rourke. 2009. Commodity Market Disintegration in the Interwar Period. NBER Working Paper No. 14767. Cambridge, MA: National Bureau of Economic Research.

Irwin, Douglas A. 1996. *Against the Tide: An Intellectual History of Free Trade*. Princeton, NJ: Princeton University Press.

Irwin, Douglas A. 1998. Changes in U.S. Tariffs: The Role of Import Prices and Commercial Policies. *American Economic Review* 88:1015–1026.

Irwin, Douglas A. 2009. *Free Trade under Fire*. 3rd ed. Princeton, NJ: Princeton University Press.

Irwin, Douglas A. 2010a. Did France Cause the Great Depression? NBER Working Paper No. 16350. Cambridge, MA: National Bureau of Economic Research.

Irwin, Douglas A. 2010b. Trade Restrictiveness and Deadweight Losses from U.S. Tariffs. *American Economic Journal: Economic Policy* 2:111–133.

Irwin, Douglas A. 2011. *Peddling Protectionism: Smoot-Hawley and the Great Depression*. Princeton, NJ: Princeton University Press.

Irwin, Douglas A., and Randall S. Kroszner. 1999. Interests, Institutions, and Ideology in Securing Policy Change: The Republican Conversion to Trade Liberalization after Smoot-Hawley. *Journal of Law & Economics* 42:643–673.

Irwin, Douglas A., Petros C. Mavroidis, and Alan O. Sykes. 2008. *The Genesis of the GATT*. New York: Cambridge University Press.

Ito, Takatoshi, Kunio Okina, and Juro Teranishi. 1993. News and the Dollar/Yen Exchange Rate, 1931–1933: The End of the Gold Standard, Imperialism, and the Great Depression. *Journal of the Japanese and International Economies* 7:107–131.

Jacks, David S., Christopher M. Meissner, and Dennis Novy. 2011. Trade Booms, Trade Busts, and Trade Costs. *Journal of International Economics* 83:185–201.

James, Harold. 1986. *The German Slump: Politics and Economics, 1924–1936*. Oxford: Clarendon Press.

James, Harold. 2001. *The End of Globalization*. Cambridge: Harvard University Press.

Johnson, H. Clark. 1997. *Gold, France, and the Great Depression, 1919–1932*. New Haven, CT: Yale University Press.

Kee, Hiau Looi, Cristina Neagu, and Alessandro Nicita. 2010. Is Protectionism on the Rise? Assessing National Trade Policies during the Crisis of 2008. World Bank Policy Research Working Paper 5274.Washington, DC: World Bank.

Keynes, John Maynard. 1919. The Economic Consequences of the Peace. In *Collected Writings of John Maynard Keynes*, 2: 148–149. London: Macmillan, for the Royal Economic Society, 1971–1988.

Keynes, John Maynard. 1923. A Tract on Monetary Reform. Vol. 4 of *Collected Writings of John Maynard Keynes* London: Macmillan, for the Royal Economic Society, 1971–1988..

Keynes, John Maynard. 1925. The Economic Consequences of Mr. Churchill. In *Collected Writings of John Maynard Keynes*, 9:220. London: Macmillan, for the Royal Economic Society, 1971–1988.

Keynes, John Maynard. 1931a. Proposal for a Revenue Tariff. In *Collected Writings of John Maynard Keynes*, 9:235. London: Macmillan, for the Royal Economic Society, 1971–1988.

Keynes, John Maynard. 1931b. We Must Restrict our Imports. In *Collected Writings of John Maynard Keynes*, 9:241. London: Macmillan, for the Royal Economic Society, 1971–1988.

Keynes, John Maynard. 1936. *The General Theory of Employment, Interest, and Money*. New York: Harcourt Brace & Co.

Keynes, John Maynard. 1971–1988. *Collected Writings of John Maynard Keynes.* London: Macmillan, for the Royal Economic Society.

Kindleberger, Charles P. 1934. Competitive Currency Deprecation between Denmark and New Zealand. *Harvard Business Review* 12:416–426.

Kindleberger, Charles P. 1986. *The World in Depression.* Rev. ed. Berkeley and Los Angeles: University of California Press.

Kindleberger, Charles P. 1989. Commercial Policy between the Wars. In *The Cambridge Economic History of Europe*, vol. 8, *The Industrial Economies: The Development of Economic and Social Policies*, ed. Peter Mathias and Sidney Pollard. New York: Cambridge University Press.

Klein, Michael W., and Jay C. Shambaugh. 2006. Fixed Exchange Rates and Trade. *Journal of International Economics* 70:359–383.

Kottman, Richard N. 1968. *Reciprocity and the North American Triangle, 1932–1938.* Ithaca, NY: Cornell University Press.

Krugman, Paul. 1982. The Macroeconomics of Protection with a Floating Exchange Rate. *Carnegie-Rochester Series on Public Policy* 16:141–182.

League of Nations. 1927. *Tariff Level Indices.* Geneva: League of Nations.

League of Nations. 1931. *Evolution of Economic and Commercial Policy (Autonomous, Contractual and Collective) Since the Tenth Assembly.* Geneva: League of Nations.

League of Nations. 1932. *World Economic Survey 1931/32.* Geneva: League of Nations.

League of Nations. 1933. *World Economic Survey 1932/33.* Geneva: League of Nations.

League of Nations. 1935. *Enquiry into Clearing Agreements.* Geneva: League of Nations.

League of Nations. 1938. *Report on Exchange Control.* Geneva: League of Nations.

League of Nations. 1939a. *Review of World Trade.* Geneva: League of Nations.

League of Nations. 1939b. *World Economic Survey 1938/39.* Geneva: League of Nations.

League of Nations. 1939c. *World Production and Prices 1938/39.* Geneva: League of Nations.

League of Nations. 1940. *Statistical Yearbook of the League of Nations, 1939/40.* Geneva: League of Nations.

League of Nations. 1942a. *Commercial Policy in the Interwar Period: International Proposals and National Policies.* Geneva: League of Nations.

League of Nations. 1942b. *Network of World Trade.* Geneva: League of Nations.

Leith-Ross, Frederick. 1968. *Money Talks: Fifty Years of International Finance.* London: Hutchison.

Lewis, W. Arthur. 1981. The Rate of Growth of World Trade, 1830–1973. In *The World Economic Order: Past and Prospects,* ed. Sven Grassman and Erik Lundberg. New York: St. Martin's Press.

Little, I. M. D., Richard N. Cooper, W. Max Corden, and Sarath Rajapatirana. 1993. *Boom, Crisis, Adjustment: The Macroeconomic Experience of Developing Countries.* New York: Oxford University Press.

Lopez-Cordova, J. Ernesto, and Christopher M. Meissner. 2003. Exchange-Rate Regimes and International Trade: Evidence from the Classical Gold Standard Era. *American Economic Review* 93:344–353.

MacDougall, Donald, and Rosemary Hutt. 1954. Imperial Preference: A Quantitative Analysis. *Economic Journal* 64: 233–257.

Maddison, Angus. 2010. Statistics on World Population, GDP and Per Capita GDP, 1–2008 AD. http://www.ggdc.net/MADDISON/Historical_Statistics/horizontal-file_02-2010.xls.

Madsen, Jakob B. 2001. Trade Barriers and the Collapse of World Trade during the Great Depression. *Southern Economic Journal* 67:848–868.

Marrison, Andrew. 2000. Legacy: War Aftermath and the End of the Nineteenth Century Liberal Trading Order, 1914–1932. In *The First World War and the International Economy,* ed. C. J. Wrigley. Northhampton, MA: Edward Elgar.

McDonald, Judith, Anthony Patrick O'Brien, and Colleen Callahan. 1997. Trade Wars: Canada's Reaction to the Smoot-Hawley Tariff. *Journal of Economic History* 57:802–826.

Meade, James E. 1948. Financial Policy and the Balance of Payments. *Economica* 15:101–115.

Meade, James E. 1955. The Case for Variable Exchange Rates. *Three Banks Review* 27:3–27. Reprinted in *The Collected Papers of James Meade,* ed. Susan Howson. Boston: Unwin & Hyman, 1988.

Meade, James E. 1978. The Meaning of "Internal Balance." *Economic Journal* 88:423–435.

Metzler, Mark. 2006. *Lever of Empire: The International Gold Standard and the Crisis of Liberalism in Postwar Japan*. Berkeley and Los Angeles: University of California Press.

Michaely, Michael, Demetris Papageorgiou, and Armeane M. Choksi. 1991. *Liberalizing Foreign Trade: Lessons of Experience in the Developing World*. Cambridge: Basil Blackwell.

Middleton, Roger. 2010. British Monetary and Fiscal Policy in the 1930s. *Oxford Review of Economic Policy* 26:414–441.

Milward, Alan S. 1981. The Reichsmark Bloc and the International Economy. In *Der "Führerstaat": Mythos und Realität. Studien zur Struktur und Politik des Dritten Reiches*, ed. Gerhard Hisrschfeld and Lothar Kettenacker. Stuttgart: Klett-Cotta.

Mitchell, Brian R. 2007. *International Historical Statistics: Europe, 1750–2005*. 6th ed. New York: Palgrave Macmillan.

Mints, Lloyd. 1950. *Monetary Policy for a Competitive Society*. New York: McGraw-Hill.

Moggridge, Donald. 1986. Keynes and the International Monetary System, 1909–46. In *International Problems and Supply-Side Economics*, ed. Jon S. Cohen and G. C. Harcourt. London: Macmillan.

Moggridge, Donald. 1992. *Maynard Keynes: An Economist's Biography*. New York: Routledge.

Mouré, Kenneth. 1991. *Managing the Franc Poincaré: Economic Understanding and Political Constraint in French Monetary Policy, 1928–1936*. New York: Cambridge University Press.

Mouré, Kenneth. 2002. *The Gold Standard Illusion: France, the Bank of France, and the International Gold Standard, 1914–1939*. New York: Oxford University Press.

Mundell, Robert A. 2000. A Reconsideration of the Twentieth Century. *American Economic Review* 90:327–340.

Neal, Larry. 1979. The Economics and Finance of Bilateral Clearing Agreements: Germany, 1934-38. *Economic History Review* 32:391–404.

Nurkse, Ragnar. 1944 *The Interwar Currency Experience*. Geneva: League of Nations.

Obstfeld, Maurice, Jay C. Shambaugh, and Alan M. Taylor. 2004. Monetary Sovereignty, Exchange Rates, and Capital Controls: The Trilemma in the Interwar Period. *IMF Staff Papers* 51:75–108.

Obstfeld, Maurice, and Alan M. Taylor. 1998. The Great Depression as a Watershed: International Capital Mobility over the Long Run. In *The Defining Moment: The Great Depression and the American Economy in the Twentieth Century*, ed. Michael D. Bordo, Claudia Goldin, and Eugene N. White. Chicago: University of Chicago Press.

Ohlin, Bertil. 1927. The Plea for Freer Trade. In *The Economic Consequences of the League*. London: Routledge.

Ohlin, Bertil. 1929. A Road to Freer Trade. Svenska Handelsbanken. *Index* 4:2–9.

Ohlin, Bertil. 1931. *Course and Phases of the World Economic Depression*. Geneva: League of Nations.

Ohlin, Bertil. 1935. International Trade and Monetary Policy. Svenska Handelsbanken. *Index* 10:155–165.

Ohlin, Bertil. 1936. Can the Gold Bloc Learn from the Sterling Bloc's Experiences? Svenska Handelsbanken. *Index* 11:51–72.

Ohlin, Bertil. 1937. Mechanisms and Objectives of Exchange Control. *American Economic Review* 27:141–150.

Ohlin, Bertil. 1945. Future Prospects and Desiderata in Commercial Policy. *Skandinaviska Banken*, April, 35–39.

Padoa-Schioppa, Tommaso. 1988. The European Monetary System: A Long-term View. In *The European Monetary System*, ed. Francesco Giavazzi, Stefano Micossi, and Marcus Miller. New York: Cambridge University Press.

Ritschl, Albrecht O. 2001. Nazi Economic Imperialism and the Exploitation of the Small: Evidence from Germany's Secret Foreign Exchange Balances, 1938–1940. *Economic History Review* 54:324–345.

Ritschl, Albrecht O. 2004. Spurious Growth in German Output Data, 1913–1938. *European Review of Economic History* 8:201–208.

Robbins, Lionel. 1934. *The Great Depression*. London: Macmillan.

Robinson, Joan. 1937. Beggar-my-Neighbor Remedies for Unemployment. In *Essays in the Theory of Employment*. New York: Macmillan.

Romer, Christina D. 1992. What Ended the Great Depression? *Journal of Economic History* 52:757–784.

Romer, Christina D. 1993. The Nation in Depression. *Journal of Economic Perspectives* 7:19–40.

Romer, Christina D., and David H. Romer. 1994. What Ends Recessions? In *NBER Macroeconomics Annual*, ed. Stanley Fischer and Julio J. Rotemberg. Cambridge, MA: MIT Press.

Salmon, Patrick. 2003. Paternalism or Partnership? Finance and Trade in Anglo-Danish Relations in the 1930s. In *Britain and Denmark: Political, Economic and Cultural Relations in the 19th and 20th Centuries*, ed. Jorgen Sevaldsen. Copenhagen: Museum Tusculanum Press.

Sayers, R. S. 1976. *The Bank of England, 1891–1944*. 2 vols. New York: Cambridge University Press.

Schacht, Hjalmar. 1934. German Trade and German Debts. *Foreign Affairs* 13:1–5.

Schatz, Howard J., and David G. Tarr. 2002. Exchange Rate Overvaluation and Trade Protection. In *Development, Trade, and the WTO: A Handbook*, ed. Bernard Hoekman, Aaditya Mattoo, and Philip English. Washington, DC: World Bank.

Scroggs, William O. 1933. Depreciated Currencies and World Trade. *Foreign Affairs* 11:513–516.

Shah Mohammed, S. I., and Jeffrey G. Williamson. 2004. Freight Rates and Productivity Gains in British Tramp Shipping, 1869–1950. *Explorations in Economic History* 8:125–147.

Straumann, Tobias. 2009. Rule Rather Than Exception: Brüning's Fear of Devaluation in Comparative Perspective. *Journal of Contemporary History* 44:603–617.

Straumann, Tobias. 2010. *Fixed Ideas: Small States and Exchange Rate Regimes in Twentieth Century Europe*. New York: Cambridge University Press.

Supple, Barry. 1959. *Commercial Crisis and Change in England, 1600–1642: A Study in the Instability of a Mercantile Economy*. Cambridge: Cambridge University Press.

Tasca, Henry J. 1938. *The Reciprocal Trade Policy of the United States*. Philadelphia: University of Pennsylvania Press.

Temin, Peter. 1989. *Lessons from the Great Depression*. Cambridge, MA: MIT Press.

Temin, Peter. 1993. The Transmission of the Great Depression. *Journal of Economic Perspectives* 7: 87–102.

Temin, Peter. 2008. The German Crisis of 1931: Evidence and Tradition. *Cliometrica* 2:5–17.

Temin, Peter, and Barrie Wigmore. 1990. End to One Big Deflation. *Explorations in Economic History* 27:483–502.

Tobin, James. 1977. How Dead Is Keynes? *Economic Inquiry* 15:459–468.

Tooze, J. Adam. 2007. *Wages of Destruction: the Making and Breaking of the Nazi Economy.* New York: Viking.

United Nations. 1962. International Trade Statistics 1900–1960. http://unstats.un.org/unsd/trade/imts/historical_data.htm.

U.S. Department of Commerce. 1976. *Historical Statistics of the United States.* Washington, DC: GPO.

Viner, Jacob. 1937. *Studies in the Theory of International Trade.* New York: Harper & Brothers.

Vines, David. 2003. John Maynard Keynes 1937–1946: The Creation of International Macroeconomics. *Economic Journal* 113:F338–F361.

Wandschneider, Kirsten. 2008. The Stability of the Interwar Gold Standard: Did Politics Matter? *Journal of Economic History* 68:151–181.

Wei, Shang-Jin, and Zeiwei Zhang. 2007. Collateral Damage: Exchange Controls and International Trade. *Journal of International Money and Finance* 26:841–863.

Whittlesey, C. R. 1937. Import Quotas in the United States. *Quarterly Journal of Economics* 52:37–65.

Wigmore, Barrie A. 1987. Was the Bank Holiday of 1933 Caused by a Run on the Dollar? *Journal of Economic History* 47:739–755.

Williamson, Phillip. 1992. *National Crisis and National Government: British Politics, the Economy, and Empire, 1926–1932.* New York: Cambridge University Press.

Wilson, Charles. 1949. Treasure and Trade Balances: The Mercantilist Problem. *Economic History Review* 2:152–161.

Wolf, Holger C., and Tarik M. Yousef. 2007. Breaking the Fetters: Why Did Countries Exit the Interwar Gold Standard? In *The New Comparative Economic History: Essays in Honor of Jeffrey G. Williamson,* ed. Timothy J. Hatton, Kevin H. O'Rourke, and Alan M. Taylor. Cambridge, MA: MIT Press.

Wolf, Nikolaus. 2007. Should I Stay or Should I Go? Understanding Poland's Adherence to Gold, 1928–1936. *Historical Social Research* 32:351–368.

Wolf, Nikolaus. 2008. Scylla and Charybdis. Explaining Europe's Exit from Gold, January 1928–December 1936. *Explorations in Economic History* 45:383–401.

Wolf, Nikolaus, and Albrecht O. Ritschl. 2011. Endogeneity of Currency Areas and Trade Blocs: Evidence from the Interwar-Period. *Kyklos* 64: 291–312.

World Trade Organization. 2010. *International Trade Statistics 2010*. Geneva: WTO.

Index

Printed in the United States
by Baker & Taylor Publisher Services